HOW TO SHOOT BETTER VIDEO

Especially for VHS, Beta and 8mm Cameras

by Robert Hirschman & Richard Procter

HAL LEONARD BOOKS

Library of Congress Catalog Card Number: 85-50894
ISBN: 0-88188-300-X

Published by: Hal Leonard Publishing Corporation, P.O. Box 13819, 8112 West Bluemound Road, Milwaukee, WI 53213 U.S.A.

First edition printed June, 1985
Revised edition printed August, 1988

INTRODUCTION

Video cameras are sweeping the country. . . and it's no passing fad! Ever since the invention of the still camera in the mid-1800's, recording images of family and friends has been an enduring and growing pastime. What better reminders of past joys and memories than photographs of the people and events which richly decorate our past.

What can be better than a photograph? A moving, talking, action-packed picture! But up to now, we've been limited to expensive and cumbersome movie cameras, projectors, screens and costly film.

The video camera has changed all that. And the current state of video development has given us the camcorder. . .camera and recorder combined in one unit. No more film to buy, shoot, take to the drug store for processing, edit, and thread into the projector; no more setting up the screen and turning down the lights, only to "enjoy" for 3 whole minutes (not to mention tearing it all down and putting it away). No wonder super 8 film cameras never really caught on!

But that's all behind us. Now we've got easy-to-use, point-and shoot video cameras. Just shoot, pop the cassette into the VCR and, voila, instantaneous playback! For the first time, moving picture photography is open to everyone.

If you'd prefer to create moving-picture memories instead of snapshots, VIDEO AND THIS BOOK, ARE FOR YOU!

If you enjoy being creative with a camera, VIDEO AND THIS BOOK ARE FOR YOU!

If you enjoy recording family events, VIDEO AND THIS BOOK are for you!

If you'd enjoy creating your own television shows, VIDEO AND THIS BOOK ARE FOR YOU!

The exciting development of home video cameras and recorders has opened a whole new world of photographic creativity to millions of men, women, and children just like you. But if your experience has been limited to still photographs and snapshots, you'll need to learn some of the basic rules of video to create interesting, informative and entertaining videos. Nothing can be more boring to an audience than watching a video made by simply turning on the camera and following the action in one long take.

As a video-maker, your goal should be to communicate in an interesting and entertaining manner. To do so, you'll need to change the way you think about photography, and in the process, learn a few simple rules.

When shooting snapshots, your concern has always been "catching the moment." The "moment" must tell the whole story, or as much of it as you can capture. That's snapshot thinking. Video is different. With video, you "catch the action." Your story unfolds from scene to scene in one seamless web.

Why learn the simple rules of video? The quality of home video equipment and tape now rivals broadcast quality television programming. From an equipment standpoint, your audience won't be able to tell the difference between your productions and professional TV shows. If the quality of your hardware compares favorably with the professionals, you'll need to know how professionals *produce* interesting, entertaining and informative television. And when you do, your audiences will keep coming back for more...while you have more and more fun producing each new video.

In writing this book, our goal has been to introduce the essential ingredients of good video on a chapter-by-chapter basis. Each chapter introduces and explains a new concept. By the time you've read this short book, you'll have all the basics you need to get started...and to have fun. Read on. Learn. Enjoy. And welcome to the wonderful world of video. It's easy and fun!

ACKNOWLEDGEMENTS

No book gets from the idea stage to the printed page without some valuable assistance from "unsung" heros and heroines.

Therefore, the authors would like to thank Jim Staublin for the "seed" and Don Farr who offered the initial input to get started in the right direction - and stay on the right track.

Glenda Herro and Dave Riggs for their ongoing encouragement and editorial direction. Their ideas and enthusiasm made not only for an enjoyable writing experience, but also for a better book.

Ray Jacobs for his insightful comments and for his graphic design ideas.

Erik Nelson, a video pro, who wouldn't stop hounding us until we got it right.

Sharon Martin for her busy fingers which touched the keyboard as fast as greased lightning; and, for her cheerful manner and smile throughout the ordeal.

And thanks to the friends who took the time and trouble to read the manuscript and make helpful comments.

Finally, a special thanks to Keith Mardak, who believed in this project enough to commit substantial dollars to it.

TABLE OF CONTENTS

Quick Start

Basic Equipment

The Language of Video

Story-Telling

Expanding the Language

Composition

Point of Reference

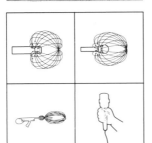

Sound

Lighting

QUICK START

**YOU'RE TEN MINUTES AWAY
FROM YOUR FIRST VIDEO!**

How To Shoot Better Video was written to give you a basic, yet in-depth look at video-making. The book is organized so that each chapter introduces new concepts and explains them in easy-to-understand, non-technical language.

This chapter, however, will get you started quickly. It provides you with an overview of all the basics you'll need to make informative, exciting, and interesting videos. You can use the information in this chapter to get you started, and as a review once you've completed the book.

Video-making is a creative, fun-filled activity. There are very few rules to follow. By learning the basics, you'll make videos which hold the attention of your audience and keep them coming back for more.

Set Your Goal

In making a video, your goal should be to communicate a story or message. Every good story has a beginning, a middle and an end. Even taping a family dinner party will be a more interesting video to watch if you think of it as a "story" with beginning, middle and end.

Before you start shooting, you should plan your shoot. By answering these questions, you can develop a production plan. What is the *main purpose* of this video? Is it to show the family trip to Disneyland? To show Henry and Bertha's wedding? To show Timmy playing little league? What is the main purpose?

Who is your audience? Will it be the family? A high school class? The members of your video club? Who is your audience?

How will you begin? Every production must begin with an establishing shot. It shows the audience where the action is taking place and who the principal participants are.

What is the *length* of the video? Keep in mind that audiences get bored watching a long video unless there's a story line running through it. Most of your videos will be of "happenings" — an event such as a family party, a little league game, the family Christmas, etc. - events that you record as they happen. "Happenings" generally have little story line, so keep them short to retain your audience's attention. 10-20 minutes is a good length.

Individual Shots —
The Building Blocks

If your picture-taking experience has been limited to still photography, you're accustomed to telling a story by "catching the moment" with individual shots. Video-making is also made up of individual shots. They are:

Long Shot

Shows the subject in full length. The subject could be a person, place or thing. Long Shots are referred to as Establishing Shots. They tell the viewer where you are and who the principal participants are. A full shot of a New York City street is an example of an Establishing Shot. It shows New York as the setting for the story. Likewise, a full shot of the Sheriff will establish him as one of the principal participants in the video.

Long Shot

Medium Shot

Concentrates the audience's attention on the most important aspect of the subject. A shot from head to waist is a good example — it shows the most important part of a person. Medium Shots are normally used to get in close to the action. A Medium Shot of the Sheriff talking to the Villain brings the viewer into the action.

Medium Shot

Close Shot

Concentrates on a single feature of the subject. A hand, a football, a tight shot of the subject's head, are all examples. A Close Shot adds color, description and explanation to your story. A Close Shot of the Sheriff's gun tells the audience a great deal about the Sheriff.

Close Shot

Cutting & Linking

Here's where video differs from still photography. While still photography is a number of loosely connected photos, video stories are told by means of cutting from one shot to another and then linking all the shots together in one, seamless web.

Here's how to use individual shots and then link them together:

First, use the Long Shot to begin your story. It tells the audience where you are. And use the Long Shot to introduce the actors or participants. The Establishing Long Shot gets your audience involved in the story and tells them where the action is.

From there, tell your story by cutting between Medium, Close and Long Shots. You'll probably use the Medium Shot more than any other. It focuses the audience's attention on the most impor-tant part of the subject. It also concentrates on the action taking place. Cut to the Close Shot to add description and detail.

Each "cut to" the next shot is a link, and together, forms the seamless web which is your story. Building a story is just like building a house. The Establishing Shot is your foundation. Then you pile shot upon shot to build your story. Follow the rule, "establish and build." Make certain that the next shot relates to the last, and provides a foundation for the following shot. Establish and build!

When cutting from shot to shot, re-member *continuity*. If your subject was walking across the camera viewfinder, right to left in the first shot, make sure you don't change your camera angle in the next shot so that he's now walking left to right. This will confuse your audience.

Techniques

You'll be able to create stories just by linking the individual Long, Medium and Close Shots. But to add spice and interest to your videos, use some of the other video tools available to you.

Pan

Follow the action from a fixed camera position by moving the camera right to left, or left to right. You may also use a Pan to take in a subject that is larger than your widest angle lens position can include in one fixed shot.

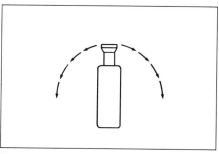

Pan

Tilt

A Tilt is nothing more than a vertical Pan. Use it to show how "tall" a tall building is. Or, use it to show presents under the Christmas tree; then, by tilting up, to show the tree decorations, and finally, up to the star on top.

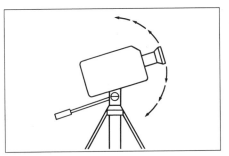

Tilt

Zoom

A Zoom Lens is really many lenses rolled into one. The lens can be used at a set position at each focal length, or, by Zooming in or out, during one long continuous shot. A Zoom In can be used as a substitute for a cut from a Long Shot to a Medium or Close Shot. A Zoom Out can be used as a substitute for a cut from a Close or Medium Shot to a Long Shot. Remember that Zoom Shots require accurate focusing and a steady camera. Use a tripod or brace your camera arm against a solid support.

Rule of Thirds

Diagonal Shot of City Street

Composing & Angles

Every good video director follows the Rules of Composition. They are:

Rule of Thirds

Divide the viewfinder into thirds, both horizontally and vertically, and fill the frame so that the subjects are balanced. A balanced composition creates a pleasing picture.

Diagonals

Are more pleasing than horizontals or verticals. If you can compose your frame by emphasizing diagonals, you'll create a more pleasing picture.

Camera Angles

You'll normally shoot from the standing position. Try varying the camera angle to shoot from down low looking up, and from up high, looking down. Looking up emphasizes height, while shooting down tends to make objects look smaller. Angles can be used to create the effects you want.

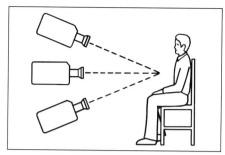

Camera Angles

Camera Position

You normally shoot at a 90-degree angle to your subject. But try placing your camera in different positions in relation to the subject. This will help keep the attention of your audience and make for a more interesting video.

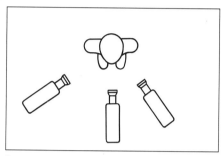

Camera Positions

Light & Sound

Whether shooting indoors or out, you'll need an adequate amount of lighting to illuminate your subjects so that your camera can "see" the action.

Indoor (or artificial) light can be supplied from a variety of sources. The key is having enough light to record a bright, sharp, colorful image on tape. Quartz light guns are handy. Powerful household bulbs can often provide adequate light. If you're shooting indoors during the day, try window light.

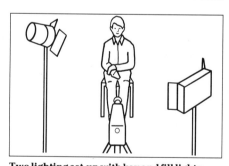

Two lighting set-up with key and fill lights

Shooting outdoors will almost always result in a clear, bright, colorful picture. When the sun is out, watch for harsh shadows. These can be avoided by use of a fill light from the quartz gun or from a reflector. Hazy, cloudy days provide even, shadowless, flattering light.

Use of fill light outdoors

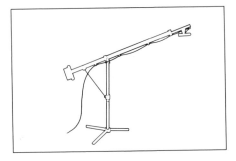

Video cameras come with a variety of microphones. Some are "omnidirectional" (pick up sounds from all directions) while others are "unidirectional" (pick up sound from straight ahead). For taping a subject at a distance, it's better to use a unidirectional mike. Better yet, use an off-camera mike placed close to the subject, connected to the camera by means of the external input jack. Controlling sound is one of the most difficult aspects of video taping. Most all built-in microphones are equipped with an automatic level control which "hears" virtually any sound within range, up to 20 feet away. Be especially careful that unwanted, extraneous sounds do not drown out your subjects.

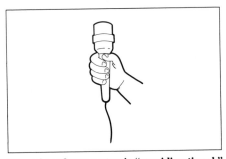

The microphone on top is "omnidirectional," while the two beneath are "unidirectional."

Directing

As the video-maker, you are responsible for producing an interesting, informative and entertaining video. By planning the production and then directing the participants through a win-win experience, everyone will have fun. As a director, you must *be prepared* so that everyone has confidence in you. *Be specific* in your requests. People have a natural desire to help you. Tell them exactly what you want. Since you're the leader, *be enthusiastic.* Enthusiasm and fun are catching. Get everyone involved. People naturally want to participate, not stand on the sidelines. Participation makes the production a joint creative effort.

Dodge City Story Outline

The story is set in the old West town of Dodge City. It illustrates the triumph of good over evil.

The action takes place at high noon, on Main Street.

The principal characters, Sheriff Jim Kincaid and Evil Rance Devlin, will be acting a six-gun shoot-out.

The finished production will have a running time of approximately ten minutes.

The principal characters will be dressed in cowboy outfits, complete with cowboy hats and boots.

In addition to the principal characters, five or six costumed extras are required to play the townspeople.

Props will include four holstered six-guns, a 5-point "Sheriff's" star, and an old time, pendulum clock.

Technical equipment will include one video camera, one portable video recorder, one television monitor, two portable battery packs, one tripod, and one portable fill light or reflector.

Technical personnel will include camera man/director, a costume person, an assistant director and a lighting/continuity assistant. The extras will double as technical crew.

Using The Camera

A shaky picture is your enemy. Keep the camera steady by using a tripod or monopod. If you don't have one available, prop your camera arm against a steady support, especially during Long Takes and Close Shots when camera shake is really noticeable.

Before you begin shooting important events, learn where all the camera controls are located so you don't have to stop shooting to find a button or switch . . . and possibly miss the action. Be sure and read the owner's manual included with the camera.

Use the Pause Control on the camera for In-Camera Editing. But remember that In-Camera Editing requires that you plan your video before you start shooting. Make up a short story outline which will guide you from start to finish. The outline is simply a summary of the most important aspects of your video. It answers the all-important "who, what, when, where, why and how" questions. Ask yourself these questions when planning each of your important videos. Advance planning will ensure a smooth, successful, fun-filled shoot.

In directing your own production, good planning is essential. The preparation of a story outline like the one shown here will help to ensure that all important details are covered.

BASIC EQUIPMENT

WHAT YOU NEED TO GET STARTED

The ultimate bargain in video is quality. Whatever equipment you choose, it should provide years of enjoyment and trouble-free use. When shopping for video equipment, take your time, read magazine ads and reviews, ask your friends, and find a dealer with knowledgeable salespeople, a good service department, and a reputation for customer satisfaction. The purchase of sophisticated electronic equipment requires more than price considerations. "You get what you pay for"—not only in terms of the equipment, but in dealer support and service.

There are three essential elements at the heart of any video system: *the recorder/player, the camera,* and *the television receiver.* Using just these three elements, you can produce a wide variety of interesting, informative, exciting and enthralling video productions.

Here are some general guidelines and tips on choosing the right equipment for you.

Choosing a Camcorder

A video camcorder is at the heart of any system. Any good camera should produce a sharp image, provide good color reproduction, capture fast-moving objects, and record at low light levels. Technical advances have come fast and furious in recent years — most importantly, in reduced size and weight, added "point and shoot" features, and in the development of more light-sensitive solid state chip imagers. Today's camcorders are half the size, half the weight, and twice as light sensitive as even recent predecessors.

1. Viewfinder

The viewfinder is the means by which you see the scene you are taping. Just a few years ago the electronic viewfinder was an uncommon extra. But today, most camcorders come equipped with an electronic viewfinder as a standard feature, although optical viewfinders are still available on less expensive models.

Through an optical viewfinder, you actually see the subject "live." But since an electronic viewfinder is really a miniature TV screen, you view your subject through an electronic viewfinder as if it were on TV. For that reason, cameras equipped with electronic viewfinders are preferable. By previewing each scene through an electronic viewfinder, you can set up and adjust props, settings and actors exactly as they'll appear on the screen in the finished product. And electronic viewfinders, operating as miniature TV's, permit you to review scenes just taped without the necessity of dragging a TV set along to your location shoots.

Electronic viewfinders are available in color and in black-and-white. Color viewfinders, like color TV's, require more electronics, are larger and are therefore more expensive.

Some experts say that a black-and-white viewfinder is preferable anyway because it allows the camera operator to concentrate on picture composition and the acting performance without the distractions of color.

If you're considering a camera with an optical viewfinder, be aware that there are two types available: The *rangefinder*—you see the scene through a separate finder located just above or beside the lens; and a *through-the-lens viewfinder* where, through a series of mirrors, you actually see right through the lens, just as in a 35 mm TTL camera.

In addition to permitting a view of the scene, viewfinders provide a host of other valuable information. Indicators in the viewfinder may show when the camera is recording, when the batteries are low, when an object is out of focus, and when the white balance is incorrect. The viewfinder will also reveal when the character generator, date-time and other built-in special effects are in use.

2. The Lens

Modern optics are sharp, bright, clear, and inexpensive. In choosing a camcorder, you should consider lens speed, focal range and macro capability.

Lens speed (measured by aperture or opening; fl.2, fl.4, fl.8, etc., are said to be "fast") is directly related to the minimum amount of light required for the camera to "see" an image. The human eye can only see an object on which light shines. Even a five-foot stack of gold bars cannot be seen in a pitch black room. But by gradually adding light, a minimum illumination level will soon be achieved. At the minimum level, you will be able to see the gold bars. And so it is with a lens. The wider the aperture (fl.2 being the widest or fastest now commercially available), the less illumination the lens (and camera) requires to "see." However, wider apertures do add to the cost of your camera.

Next, consider the focal range or zooming ratio of the lens. All Zoom Lenses go from wide-angle to telephoto. But how wide is wide? And how narrow is telephoto?

The lens angle of view is measured in millimeters — the lower the number (5mm, 6mm, 7mm, etc.) the wider the angle. Conversely, the higher the number (40mm, 45mm, 50mm, etc.) the narrower the angle or longer the telephoto. Manufacturers rate Zoom Lenses as ratios, e.g., 6:1, 7:1, 10:1, etc. If the wide-angle is 7mm and the telephoto is

42mm, the lens is rated as 6:1. Zoom Lenses may be operated manually or by means of a small motor in the camera. A motorized Zoom ensures smooth, even, continuous Zoom Shots.

A Macro Lens permits close focusing on a small subject, much like a microscope or magnifying glass. A macro feature on your camcorder's lens is useful in certain limited circumstances; for example, when shooting a tiny object such as a spider or the head of a penny, since the Macro permits focusing as close as one inch.

Some cameras, via an adaptor, permit the use of lenses designed for 35 mm SLR photography in place of a standard 6X or 8X Zoom Lens. This expanded range of lenses provides the camera operator with extended range telephoto and wide-angle shots not otherwise available with the standard Zoom Lens.

3. Autofocus

Many cameras come equipped with an autofocus feature. Autofocus is available in the "video-detail" design or the "infrared" design system. Video-detail is the superior design, permitting accurate focusing to infinity. Infrared is accurate only to about 35 feet. Autofocus works by focusing on the central subject in the viewfinder. Coupled to a motor, the lens automatically focuses on the central object. While autofocus has minor drawbacks (as when you don't want to focus on the central subject), it nevertheless allows you to concentrate on the creative aspects of video-making, leaving the mechanical aspects to electronic wizardry.

4. Light Sensitivity

An optical image "seen" through the camera lens is converted into electrical signals and then stored on tape for later viewing. How does the conversion take place? Two types of photoconductive surfaces are used: The *vacuum-tube pickup,* or the *solid-state electronic imager.* Tubes are large (the smallest being 1/3 inch and the largest, 2/3 inch), necessitating larger camcorders to house them. With the trend toward smaller, lighter, more portable camcorders comes development of the solid-state imager, or micro-chip. Its obvious advantage is size. The most compact camcorders use chips as photoconductors. Every year, chips have become "finer" — able to create greater detail, and so low-light sensitive that they can see better in low light than the human eye.

5. Other Features

Automatic Aperture leaves the solution of exposure problems to the camcorder — again, freeing you up to make creative decisions. But look for manual override. It adds to your creative options. In addition to features labeled as "special effects," manual override of certain automatic features provides creative, special effects possibilities. Manual override of automatic exposure, for example, provides unique Fade-In Fade-Out and silhouetting possibilities. Fade-In Fade-Out is a creative tool which also eliminates jarring scene changes. Fades are used as special effects: Fade-Outs give your video a professional look, and Fade-Ins can be used to simulate the passage of time.

The *Eyesight Correction Eyepiece* permits adjustment of the viewfinder to your own vision. It's especially useful if you wear glasses, as it permits you to shoot without your glasses and still see clearly, assuming you have no major eye deficiencies.

Auto White Balance permits color balance automatically. Better camcorders have *continuous* Automatic White Balance, which constantly monitors color temperature and automatically adjusts for the best picture. The non-continuous variety requires that you point the camcorder at a white object, activate the White Balance switch, and wait until the white balance indicator automatically adjusts itself. Non-continuous White Balance must be readjusted as lighting conditions change. Since white is an equal mixture of the primary colors — Red, Green and Blue — if the white you get is a true white (that is, it's balanced), all the other colors will be correct. A feature that balances color automatically is well worth the additional cost. As with manual override of automatic exposure and automatic focusing, manual override of Auto White Balance provides creative special effects possibilities.

A *Built-in Microphone* is usually included as a standard feature. Built-in mikes may be fixed or extendable (boom mikes); the latter permitting closer positioning to the actors. For really close mike positioning, make certain your camera has an External Mike Input Jack.

A *Standby Switch* conserves battery power by shutting off the electronic viewfinder, while leaving the tape loaded and ready to begin recording.

The *Color Temperature Switch* permits you to adjust for indoor and outdoor shooting. Light sources such as the sun, an ordinary light bulb, or a fluorescent bulb, produce different colors and therefore cast their "light" on your scene. The sun casts a "blue" light, an ordinary light bulb casts a "white" light, while a fluorescent bulb casts a "greenish" light. To compensate, use this Switch (also known as an "Indoor-Outdoor" Switch).

6. Special Features

High Speed Shutter — Many camcorders have a special switch or variable setting which allows you to shoot pictures with the specific intent to play them back at slow motion or stop action with no perceptible blur. This is particularly useful if you are using your camcorder to coach a sport or to study any fast-moving object.

Other special features include a *Date/Time Switch* (allowing you to record today's date and time on tape); a *Character Generator* (permitting you to create titles and limited special effects); *Positive/Negative Color Reversal* (for creative reverse-type special effects); with more features being continually developed.

Camcorders

The essential element of your video system is the camcorder. A camcorder is a video camera with a built-in video recorder. In other words, the video tape is inserted into the camera body, and the battery which powers the combination camera/recorder is either inserted into or attached to the camera body. Therefore, the camcorder is the only single piece of equipment you need to carry with you when you make your videos. The size and features of today's available camcorders vary to suit anyone's needs.

In recent years, the greatest emphasis on innovation in consumer electronics has been on "smallness." However, decreasing size in a camcorder is not always an advantage. Many experienced amateur videographers have a strong preference for a shoulder-resting camcorder, which enhances steadiness when shooting long segments — whether it's a dance recital, a little league ballgame, or a wedding. (Of course, there are some very compact tripods now available that are extremely sturdy and have been designed especially for videography.) Other equally experienced video users strongly prefer the smallest possible camcorder to facilitate ease of packing, traveling and using at tourist attractions. So to a large extent, the size and format of camcorder you choose should be determined by your intended use.

Camcorders are available in every video format: Beta, 8mm, VHS, Super VHS, VHS-C, and Super VHS-C. The tape formats known as "full size" are the 1/2 inch Beta, VHS, or Super VHS tapes — these are standard size cassettes which are typically used in home video recorder machines. Camcorders that use full size tapes will, of necessity, be larger camcorders. The 8mm, VHS-C, and Super VHS-C (the "C" stands for "compact") are small cassettes and allow for the construction of small camcorders.

As always, life is not so simple as to allow you to choose a camcorder by size alone; there are other advantages and disadvantages which may complement or conflict with your choice so far. For example, the full size VHS camcorders will allow you to record up to two hours on one standard size VHS cassette, while the VHS-C cassette will hold only twenty minutes of video with equivalent picture quality. In addition, the VHS-C cassette requires an adapter to enable you to play a VHS-C cassette in a VHS home VCR (such adapters are usually included with a VHS-C camcorder, but nonetheless, it is an extra mechanical device that can fail or at the least, needs to be kept track of). On the other hand, if you purchase a camcorder that has playback capability, you can play your video creations directly on most any television set, or directly into a home VCR for duplication and editing.

The 8mm format camcorders also use very small cassettes, but have the additional advantage of two hour recording capability. This cassette, however, has no adapter and must be played on an 8mm video deck or, if so equipped, played through the camcorder directly into most any TV set or into any home VCR (regardless of format). This brings up a commonly-held misconception: Regardless of the format of cassette your camcorder uses, if it has playback capability, it can be connected to any home VCR for tape copying and editing. For example, if you choose an 8mm camcorder with playback capability, it can be connected to a VHS video recorder so that you can create a VHS copy of the 8mm movie you

made. Since even after reading this book, most home videographers won't be professionals, you will want to edit out some mistakes from your home videos (or even resequence certain sections of your video), you should strongly consider the need for a camcorder with playback capability.

By now, the inevitable question has probably occurred to you: Why are there so many different video formats? There continue to be rapid advances in consumer electronics each year, with no apparent end in sight for the "ultimate" perfect TV, perfect picture, or perfect camcorder. Each video format was developed and improved from preceding technology, and every so often there is a "leap" in technology, such as 8mm or Super VHS, which creates an incompatible new format much better than its predecessor. And while the 8mm tape, by virtue of its cassette size, is obviously not going to fit into a VHS video recorder, the Super VHS recording won't fit either. A Super VHS recording is made on a tape much finer and different in coating than a standard VHS tape, although both are housed in identical style cassettes. The Super VHS recording will not play with a distinguishable picture on a standard VHS video recorder.

Using the Camcorder

While some video buffs may have movie camera experience, most video-makers will only have had still camera experience. Still cameras catch "the moment," while video cameras catch "the action." And the nature of the "shoot" (still vs. action) dictates how you handle the camcorder.

Normally, when shooting a still picture, you tense up for an instant during the shot. However, since action takes place over a period of time, you need to handle the video camera in a relaxed and fluid manner.

As soon as you get your camcorder, practice using it. Learn where the controls are. Practice using each of its features. Experiment with special effects. Stay relaxed while shooting — don't tense up. Practice steadying the camcorder. Your goal is to be at ease and comfortable while handling the camcorder.

Once the camcorder controls become second nature to you, you'll be able to concentrate on picture-taking.

Battery Power

Camcorders get their power supply from a 110-volt wall outlet or built-in battery compartment.

Batteries are of two types: *lead-acid,* which holds its charge for long periods of time when the battery is not in use, but takes a long time (up to 12 hours) to recharge; and *ni-cad,* which recharges very quickly, but rapidly loses its charge when not in use. Most camcorder manufacturers today use ni-cad batteries.

With either type of battery, maximum camcorder operating time is one hour, and probably less (40-45 minutes) under most conditions. Optional accessory batteries may be rated at two hours or more, but they add a lot of weight to the camcorder. It's better to carry at least one full-charged spare one hour battery when you're on a location shoot. If possible, save the battery by plugging into a wall outlet. And remember to bring lots of extension cords.

You may want to consider a longer duration battery belt, but even these packs can get heavy after a time.

Purchasing Video Equipment

As with all other equipment, choosing a VCR or camcorder is a very personal decision and depends on your needs and budget. After talking to your friends, reading the magazine ads and reviews, and determining how much you want to spend, find a good video dealer. Surprisingly, most video salespeople are knowledgeable and frank with their advice. Good salespeople are up-to-date on the latest product offerings. The dedicated ones read all the reviews and attend trade shows. As a result, they're well informed on all the latest features: which manufacturer has what, how it works, and how you can use it. Look for a salesperson who is geniunely interested in what he/she is doing and who wants to form a long-term relationship with you. That kind of person should serve you well. A good salesperson can help you determine your own needs and help you fill them . . . within your budget.

If possible, borrow or rent a camcorder before you buy. Try it out. Shoot a family gathering, a sporting event, a concert, a school pageant. Use all of the camcorder's features. See which ones are important to you. Look for ease of handling, picture quality, portability, color saturation, quality construction, automatic features, and operating characteristics. Just one day of "hands-on" experience will help you make the best choice.

And when you finally make your choice, study the owner's manual until you know it by heart. It's a great help to have this important information at your fingertips.

When choosing a VCR, consider the following:

1. Features

Does the VCR have all the features you need — not only for taping from the camera, but also for taping broadcasts and for showing prerecorded cassettes? Some of the features available include: freeze frame, picture search, frame by frame advance, slow motion, double speed, stereo sound, Dolby noise reduction, remote control (wireless or wired) multi-day and multi-program timers, hi-fi sound, and more. With the frantic pace of technological advances, it seems as if new features are introduced at every turn. But the basic features endure.

2. Obsolescence

Technical advances seem to make existing products obsolete. While that may appear to be true, in reality it's not true at all. Obsolescence is directly related to your needs and to the job to be done. Unless you're planning to produce professional videos, VCR's equipped with the basics should serve you well. . . now and in the future. If you're concerned about obsolescence, consult a trusted salesperson. He or she will be up on all the latest developments and what's likely to be coming down the pike.

Don't confuse obsolescence with technological advances. No matter what you buy, state-of-the-art will undoubtedly be better next year. But your equipment is obsolete only if it can't be repaired or used anymore.

A Word about Receivers/Monitors

The home TV set we've come to know and love (hate?) is called a "receiver." A receiver is distinguished from a "monitor" in that a receiver also has a tuner. Monitors have no tuners.

With recent advances in video technology, and especially since the recent public outcry for TV's with hi-fi stereo sound, manufacturers have lately taken to the introduction of "so-called" monitors. In reality, they are monitors/receivers, since they include tuners as well as video and audio inputs and outputs. In addition to providing access to well over 100 channels, stereo sound, VCR and video disk, camera inputs and outputs, this new generation of monitors features high resolution, high definition pictures, and giant screens.

Using a camera mounted on a tripod.

Using the wall to support the body while shooting.

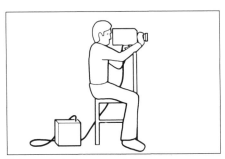

Using a chair for support.

Kneeling to support the camera.

Tripods and Steadying the Camera

Nothing is more distracting than a shaky picture. As you'll learn later on, your goal should be to rivet the audience's attention on the story, not on your camera technique... or lack of it. Shaky pictures call attention to an unsteady camera operator. Conversely, no one notices a rock-solid picture. Therefore, a tripod should be an essential part of your video equipment. Look for a well-built, solidly constructed tripod — one which will give your camera maximum support. A tripod with maximum head movement should be selected. One featuring a Pan and Tilt Head are basic. These permit vertical and horizontal movement.

A monopod (a single-legged camera support) may be more versatile and easier to handle than a tripod. Monopods are especially useful when shooting fast-moving events such as sports.

If no tripod or monopod is available, or the shooting situation precludes the use of one, steady the camera by some other method. This will usually be by means of propping yourself, your camera arm, or the camera on or against some solid support. Lean against a wall, lean on a chair, lean against a car, kneel and support your camera arm on your knee, etc. Do whatever you can to keep the camera steady.

Summary

Once you've assembled your "core" system—camcorder, monitor/receiver and tripod—you can begin to create your own video productions. As you become more involved, whether shooting family activities, shooting business presentations, or creating your own TV programs, you'll want to gradually expand your core system with "satellites." These may include a second VCR to enhance editing capabilities, an editing controller, a compatible stereo sound system, a front projection, giant-size TV monitor, a second camera and more equipment as it becomes available. As with any creative endeavor, the videomaker should have the right tools for the job.

In Videowares' *How To Shoot Better Video* book, we'll assume you are working with either a single camera and VCR or with a camcorder . . . the basic tools of the trade.

THE LANGUAGE OF VIDEO

3

"TOOLS OF THE TRADE"

Every discipline has its own "language." Doctors communicate with each other using medical terminology. Lawyers communicate using legal terminology. Carpenters and plumbers communicate with each other using that special language which describes what they do and the materials they use. And so on.

As children, we learned about building blocks. We piled block on block and assembled crude structures at first, but later built more sophisticated structures using those very same blocks.

The Parts of Speech

Later, at school, we learned about other more sophisticated types of "building blocks" — grammar and the parts of speech. The parts of speech give meaning to what we say. Our purpose in this chapter is to explain the "Language of Video." Our goal is to show you how to use these video "parts of speech" in order to create and give meaning to your video stories. You will find that by learning and practicing these "parts of speech" with your video camera, you will create more meaningful, professional and audience-pleasing video stories.

During our first years in school, we learned the basic parts of speech. Our first lesson in grammar taught us about the "noun." We learned that the noun identified the person, place, or thing in a sentence. A noun was the "subject of our interest." For example, "Sheriff" is a noun.

Next, we heard about the "verb." Now things got more interesting. The verb was the "action" word. The verb told us what was happening. It put the noun in motion. "Walks" is a verb. "Sheriff walks" tells us what the sheriff is doing and is a complete sentence.

Finally, in this basic stage of our grammatical education, we learned about "adjectives." They modify or explain the noun. Adjectives add flavor and interest to the story. "Lean," "mean," "dusty," and "brick-red" are all adjectives in the next sentence. "The lean, mean Sheriff walks down the dusty, brick-red street."

Of course, the English language is considerably more complex than these simple parts of speech. But for our purposes, we will show you a direct parallel between these basic parts of speech and the basic language of video. Keep in mind that the language of video can be as complex as our own rules of grammar. However, no matter how well you know all of the complex rules, you still cannot create a meaningful sentence without first referring to the basic rules. It is the same in the language of video.

Telling stories through pictures is as old as man himself. However, the recording of photographic images for *storytelling purposes* is a relatively new process. First came the still film camera. Next, a moving picture film camera was developed. The video camera is simply the most recent evolutionary phase of a motion picture process that began around the turn of the century. But the goal has always remained the same: *To communicate a message or tell a story.*

Early Productions

Those early "visual recording artists" way back in 1900 were trying to do the same thing you'll be doing . . . thrill and enthrall their audience through a series of recorded images which seamlessly tell a story of interest to that particular audience. The first directors — Milies in France and W.S. Porter in America — had no moving picture story language to work with. They were forced to invent the art form as they went along by simply experimenting with this technique and that. Just as the early equipment was basic, so were the productions.

At first, film productions were made inside the theater. These early directors simply bolted a camera to a chair in 12th row center, rolled the camera and yelled for "action." The camera would remain in a fixed position while the actors moved about the stage saying their lines and playing their roles. An entire 12 minute film would often be made in one long shot. As you can imagine, the

results were incredibly boring. It would be just as if you were trying to communicate with a friend using only nouns; no action words and no adjectives.

Then along came D.W. Griffith, who is revered as the father of American visual arts. What did Griffith do that was so revolutionary? For a start, he unbolted the camera and moved it around to different positions, experimenting as he went along. In so doing, he quite by accident invented the language of the visual arts that we continue to use today. In this VideoWare Series, we have adapted that language to the video camera and updated it to "the language of video."

What is this basic language of video?

Just as in basic grammar, there are three parts of video speech. They are the *Long Shot,* the *Medium Shot,* and the *Close Shot.* That's it! Your basic language of video.

Long Shot, Medium Shot, Close Shot

Let's see how the grammatical parts of speech and the language of video relate to each other. The Long Shot is similar to the noun. The Long Shot *establishes* the subject of the action. It shows the subject in full length. Some refer to it as the "Establishing" Shot. It is "what" and "where" we are talking about. Establishing Shots are important because they tell the viewer where you are; they establish your locale and get the viewer involved in the story.

The Medium Shot can be likened to the verb. Now that we have used the Long Shot to establish the subject, we use the Medium Shot to "see" the action. It provides us with the reason for our interest in the story. It's "why" we are talking about the subject. The Medium Shot concentrates our attention on the most important aspect of the subject, as for example, a shot of the subject from head to waist.

Finally, we use the Close Up or Close Shot to add description, color, and explanation to the subject. It is the adjective. The Close Up adds spice and interest to the story. It concentrates on a single feature of the subject, as for example, a Close Shot of the subject's hand on his gun.

So again, there you have it. The three basic parts of the language of video: the Long Shot, the Medium Shot, and the Close Up. Now let's explore how to use these parts of speech when creating a video story. You can use these parts of "video speech" to make your video production look more professional, more appealing, and more interesting to your audience. Here's how they can be used in a video story you might see on television.

Long Shot

Medium Shot

Close Shot

Establishing shot of Dodge City

Establishing shot of the Sheriff

Establishing shot of the Villain

Close Shot

"Shoot-Out In Dodge City"

The scene is Dodge City. This is where the action will take place. It is the subject or setting for our story. The camera is placed in a position to capture the full length of Main Street. The Long Shot establishes where we are. Remember, the Long Shot is the establishing Shot.

Our hero, Sheriff Jim Kincaid, is also revealed by means of an establishing shot. Sheriff Kincaid is revealed through the use of a full shot. . . from head to toe and in relation to his setting. Sheriff Kincaid is another subject (noun) of our story.

The Villain, Evil Rance Devlin, is revealed in yet another establishing shot. A full shot shows Evil Rance dressed in black and looking menacing. Devlin is the other subject (noun) of our story. The director calls for "action" and Evil Rance Devlin slowly looks up.

To recap, the camera has revealed a story set in Dodge City, with its principal characters, Sheriff Kincaid and the Villain Devlin. Devlin has just looked up at the clock. Something is about to happen.

Cut to a Close Up of the clock face. It's high noon. By shooting a Close Up of the clock face, the director has informed us that the time of day is important to this story. The Close Up adds spice and interest. Tension begins building.

Now, our hero, Sheriff Kincaid, also looks up at the clock. The Sheriff turns to his wife and the camera moves in for a Medium Shot. The Medium Shot shows the Sheriff and his wife talking. The action begins.

> *Sheriff:* It's time.
> *Wife:* Sure you shouldn't get some help?
> *Sheriff:* This is my battle. I've got to face him alone.

To recap, the Medium Shot was used much like the verb: to let us in closer to "see" the action.

Cut to a Close Shot of Devlin's face. Staring straight ahead, he is stern and unsmiling.

Cut to a Close Shot of the Sheriff's face. Equally stern.

> *Sheriff:* Draw!

Cut to a Medium Shot of Devlin going for his gun. As he pulls it out of his holster . . .

Cut to a Medium Shot of the Sheriff going for his gun and then taking aim. Two shots are heard.

Cut to a Long Shot. Both figures stand still for a split second. Suddenly, Devlin falls over backwards.

Cut to a Close Shot of the Sheriff's face. His stern look gives way to a tight-lipped smile. *He blows the smoke from his gun barrel.*

Cut to a Long Shot of Main Street. The Sheriff's wife, relieved and elated at her husband's victory, runs into the street to join him.

Notice what we have done in this short, but graphic scene. First, we have created a complete story with beginning, middle, and end. And we have visually told the story using just three video "parts of speech." While there are a number of other parts of "video speech" that we will learn later in this book, at this point, we have shown that it is possible to tell a complete story using just the three basic parts of visual story-telling "speech." The parallel with grammatical parts of speech is clear: You can tell a complete story by simply using nouns, verbs, and adjectives; and, you can tell a visual story simply by using the Long Shot, Medium Shot, and Close Shot. In both "languages," these are the basic building blocks of story-telling.

Summary

In this chapter on the "Language of Video," we have learned about the three basic parts of "video speech." By simply using these three basic parts, you can create a meaningful and complete video story. While there are numerous other creative video techniques, you will continually refer back to, and use, the Long Shot, Medium Shot, and Close Shot to effectively tell your video story.

STORY-TELLING

SAY IT IN PICTURES

In the last chapter, you were introduced to the basic shots which make up the language of video. But individual shots, like individual words, are not enough to tell a story. Your aim in video-making is to communicate . . . to tell a story. And good story-telling requires not only the right choice of individual words (shots), but also the artful stringing together of those words (shots) to form sentences, paragraphs, and finally, a complete story.

How does the video-maker string shots together to form meaningful sequences? In the Dodge City Shoot-Out, you probably noticed that each sentence of the script began with the words "Cut to" followed by a short description of the next shot. Each "Cut to" is a *link* to the next shot in the sequence. And each sequence links together to form the complete story.

Establish & Build

Video stories are based on the "establish and build" principle. Each "Cut to" must relate to and build on, or explain, a prior shot. In the Dodge City Shoot-Out, for example, we opened with a Long Shot of Dodge City's Main Street. We established Main Street as the locale for the action. All shots which followed were related to this establishing shot.

Early in the Dodge City story, we introduced the Villain Devlin, by means of an establishing, Full Shot. By doing so, we communicated to the audience that Devlin was to be one of the principal characters in the story. But suppose we had introduced Devlin by means of a Close Shot of him fingering his pearl-handled six-gun. The audience would have been confused, since the shot was isolated and unrelated to anything that had gone before it.

Later in this book, you'll learn more about the art of visual story-telling. But for now, think, about the "establish and build" principle. It works just like

building a house: you lay the foundation with Establishing Shots and build up the structure through the linking of Long Shots, Medium Shots, and Close Shots, until finally, your structure (story) is completed.

Many people reading this book will be new to video-making. If you've had no movie-making experience and all of your picture-taking has been on a still camera, the "establish and build" principle is all the more important to you. Still cameras "catch the moment." Each picture is a story in itself. But video cameras "catch the action." By its very nature, a video story is made up of a series or sequence of individual shots. Each shot is piled on top of the last one, and together they tell a story.

Every story has a beginning, a middle and an end. The creative linking of the Long Shot, Medium Shot, and Close Shot should begin, then unfold, and finally end your story in an interesting and meaningful way.

Remember to establish and build. Establish and build by means of the cuts to Long, Medium, and Close Shots. In the best visual story-telling, a good director (you!) may cut 30 times within a period of two minutes. To the audience, it's all one flowing "sentence," but to the storyteller, it's accomplished by means of piling one visual building block on another.

Next time you watch a story on TV, pay special attention to the Long, Medium, and Close Shots used by the director. Notice, too, the number of cuts within a two minute period of time. You'll be amazed, and you'll learn important lessons for your own video productions.

Try it Yourself

Let's practice linking the Long Shot, Medium Shot, and Close Shot in the following exercise. This exercise was designed for ease of practice. All you need is one actor and the following props: a kitchen, a loaf of bread, a kitchen clock, jar of mayonnaise, slice of cheese, knife, toaster, and plate.

In this visual exercise, you will be telling the story of "THE MAKING OF A CHEESE SANDWICH."

Open with a Long Shot of the kitchen. This is the Establishing Shot. It shows your audience where the action will take place.

Cut to a Medium Shot of the sandwich fixin's which you have previously arranged on the kitchen counter.

Cut to a Long Shot of your actor entering the kitchen. Once again, you have told us the subject of the action.

The camera continues rolling as the actor approaches the assembled ingredients.

Cut to a Medium Shot of your actor removing two slices of bread and putting them in the toaster.

Cut to a Medium Shot of your actor opening the jar of mayonnaise.

Cut to a Close Shot revealing the glowing coils of the toaster.

Cut to a Medium Shot of your actor looking up.

Cut to a Close Shot of the kitchen clock with second hand slowly turning.

Cut to a Medium Shot of your actor looking at the toaster

Cut to a Close Shot of the toaster just as the toast "pops-up."

Cut to a Medium shot of your actor removing the slices of toast, placing them on the plate, using the knife to apply mayonnaise to both slices, placing the cheese slice on the bread, placing one slice of bread on top of the other, and then cutting the sandwich in half.

Cut to a Long Shot of your actor carrying the plate to the kitchen table.

Cut to a Medium Shot of your actor taking her first bite of the sandwich.

Finally, cut to a Long Shot of your actor loading the dishwasher.

Once again, by simply cutting back and forth between the Long Shot, Medium Shot, and Close Shot, you have told a complete story.

One Plus One Equals Three - Special "Cuts"

While D.W. Griffith, by unbolting the camera and moving it around, created the visual story-telling language we use today, Sergei Eisenstein, a Russian director active in the 1920's and 1930's, discovered an interesting and useful principle. We call this the "one plus one equals three" rule, or "Eisenstein's Law." Here it is: *Two images placed next to each other will create an entirely different third image in the mind of a viewer.* For example, we see a Medium Shot of an old man, looking down.

Cut to a Medium Shot of a baby in its crib. So far, one plus one.

What was the third image created in your mind? Is the old man kindly, sympathetic, and warm-hearted?

Now, take the exact same image of the old man, smiling, looking down.

Instead of the baby carriage, cut to a photo of a magazine layout showing ladies' swimwear.

What is your third image now? Remember, we used exactly the same image of the old man in both scenes. However, what you previously saw as a kindly, sympathetic and warm-hearted old man has, no doubt, now turned into an image of a smirking, "dirty old man." "One plus one equals three."

Another example was provided in our shoot-out on Main Street. At one point, Devlin was walking up the street. The camera then cut to the Sheriff walking down the street. These shots were placed next to each other, but at no time were Devlin and the Sheriff in the same shot. Yet, you simply assumed they were walking towards each other. "One plus one equals three."

Keep "Eisenstein's Law" in mind. It is an extremely useful story-telling tool. Use the rule as you cut from scene to scene.

Now, it's time to create your own exercise using the techniques you have learned in this chapter. Put your camera down and let your imagination wander. Be creative. First, think of the story you wish to tell. Where do you want the story to take place? How many actors do you need? Do you need any props? If you are using actors, will they deliver lines? If so, what is the dialogue?

As you answer each of the questions we have posed, close your eyes and "see" the story unfolding in your imagination. When it comes time to shoot the action, simply follow the picture created in your mind. But always be alert to the spontaneity of your actors and your setting. Unexpected developments can enhance your story and often provide moments of drama, comedy, and that special touch of human emotion. *Good luck!*

Summary

In addition to the Long, Medium, and Close Shots, you must remember the relationship each shot bears to the shot before and the shot after. It is the relationship between all of the "cuts" which work together to create a seamless story.

Finally, always keep the "one plus one equals three" rule in the back of your mind for handy reference. The rule is another example of the relationship between "cuts." But avoid unintended results by pre-visualizing the "third image" created.

EXPANDING THE LANGUAGE

**PANNING, TILTING, TRACKING,
ZOOMING, & DEPTH OF FOCUS**

So far, we've learned the basic language of video. We saw that video has a set of rules for making individual shots and other rules by which numerous shots can be linked together to form a complete story.

But just as in the English language, there is more to the language of video than the Long Shot, the Medium Shot, and the Close Shot. In this chapter, we're going to expand your vocabulary.

As you learn about Panning, Tilting, Tracking, Zooming, and Depth of Focus, think of them not as exotic add-ons, but as basic tools in your repertoire. However, use them as you would salt and pepper: a dash here and a dash there, to add spice and interest to your video productions. Each of these techniques makes a statement of its own. When used appropriately, they can add expression, impact, and clarity to your story.

Panning

The opening shot of the highly acclaimed film "The Last Picture Show" is a 360-degree pan of the small Texas town in which the story is set. Most film makers would have "established" the town with a Long Shot, but the director, Peter Bogdanovich, wanted something more effective to emphasize the empty desolation of that dusty town. By using a slow Pan Shot, every member of the audience was seemingly transported right into that dusty town to experience its emptiness and desolation. This unusual Pan Shot creatively underlined an important story element in a way that no static Long Shot could possibly achieve.

Whenever your camera is in a fixed position, and you move it horizontally during a shot, left-to-right or right-to-left, you produce a Pan Shot. There are several reasons to choose a Pan rather than a static Long, Medium, or Close Shot. The most natural reason is to follow a subject from one place to another. Imagine your actor walking from one end of a long room to the other. One way to shoot him would be to pan the camera as he walks.

Pan Shots are also used to capture the sheer size of your subject: the entire length of a football stadium; a beautiful green meadow in a national park. Unless your camera has an extremely wide-angle lens, you're not going to capture the entire scene by simply pointing and shooting with a Long Shot. Panning calls attention to the fact that what you're shooting can't be contained in a single static shot. And even if it could, remember the gripping effect created by the Pan in "The Last Picture Show." By using the Pan Shot, the camera comments on the scene in a way that is not possible with the normal Long Shot.

As a rule, the Pan Shot is an effective variation on the Long Shot. Here are some tips to help you produce consistently good Pan Shots:

1. Use a tripod whenever possible. Tripods steady the camera and help you avoid annoying camera shake.

2. When using a tripod, place your body in the "finishing" position right from the start. Although somewhat uncomfortable, you'll get better looking results.

3. Hold your shot for a few seconds at the beginning and again at the end. Again, you'll get better looking results, and increase your story options at the editing table.

4. Rehearse your shot. Determine where you want to be at the start, in the middle, and at the end of the shot.

5. Always keep your camera slightly ahead of the subject as you follow his movement. This will give your subject plenty of room within the frame and will make it appear as though your subject is walking into (not out of) the shot.

6. Is the background important? If you're Panning up close to a fast moving subject (a car), for example, the background will be blurred. If the background is important, move back or use your camera's shortest focal length lens position (wide-angle) to accomplish the same result.

Tilting

A Tilt is nothing more than a vertical Pan. It's used in much the same way; as a variation or replacement for the Long Shot, it is an Establishing Shot, to give the illusion of size to your subject. For example, if you were visiting a big city and wished to communicate the size of a tall building, you would not record it with a static Long Shot. The best way to communicate the tremendous height of the building would be to begin the shot at the street level entrance and then slowly Tilt up to the very top.

All the rules of Panning apply to the Tilt Shot, plus a few more:

1. Shooting upwards accentuates height. The higher the camera angle, the more you comment on and dramatize the height. If you do not want to call too much attention to the height of the structure, move your camera position farther back from your subject.

2. Be aware of exposure problems created by pointing the camera skyward. Cameras with automatic exposure controls will adjust for the increased light and turn your beautifully photographed building into a black silhouette as you reach the top. Be especially careful not to point your camera at the sun. Even a short exposure to the sun can irreparably damage your camera's delicate tube element.

Tracking

While Panning results by following the subject from a fixed camera position, Tracking requires the camera itself to move; "tracking" the subject as he, she, or it, moves. Since Tracking simulates our normal way of "seeing" a movie (with our audience eye), it can be used as a Long Shot, Medium Shot, Close Shot, or any combination - but most commonly, Tracking is used as a Long Shot. Tracking, when done with care, adds a great deal of impact to your videos. All big budget movies (and many low budget ones) use Tracking extensively. Steven Spielberg uses it in every one of his movies. Tracking adds a real element of professionalism to your work; it adds a sense of vitality and movement. It can charge a simple monologue with excitement as the subject is presented in front of an ever-changing background.

Notice how professional film and video makers use the Tracking Shot: As a tool of "discovery," where the camera allows the audience to "discover" in the background what the characters in the foreground cannot see behind them; to "liven up" ordinary dialogue sequences - the Tracking Shot adds urgency and excitement, as where the camera races down the hall, following two interns, rushing to the emergency room, exchanging information about the patient.

Tracking, used sparingly and only when appropriate to the story, can be a valuable and effective tool. The most important rule to remember is to avoid camera shake.

Example of a tracking sequence – the camera follows the subjects to reveal their final destination.

Here are a few tips:

1. Use your camera's shortest focal length. A wide-angle lens position optically reduces the effects of camera shake.

2. Steady your camera by means of a shoulder brace, or prop your camera arm against a solid support.

3. Use a dolly (any device with wheels) to move you and the camera smoothly from one place to another. Any device that will safely support you is suitable; a child's red wagon, a furniture dolly, even a wheel chair. And Tracking from a moving car can be great fun!

4. Track over a smooth surface. A flat linoleum floor is better than a road filled with ruts.

Zooming

As you might guess, a zoom lens is required to produce a "Zoom Shot." What is a zoom lens? It's really many lenses rolled into one, from wide-angle (measured at approximately 7-10mm) to narrow-angle (also known as telephoto and measuring 40mm and up), and everything in between. Virtually every video camera manufactured today comes equipped with a zoom lens.

Knowing the *angles of view* of your lens is important. Two things happen at each extreme: In the wide-angle position, you'll get more information packed into each frame, but your subject will seem further away from the camera than it really is. That's why use of the wide-angle position reduces the visual effects of camera shake. In the narrow-angle (telephoto) position, you'll get less information into each frame, but your subject will seem closer to the camera than it really is. That's why telephoto shots magnify camera shake. The telephoto lens seems to reach out and bring everything within its view right up close, giving it an impact not otherwise obtainable.

In a "Zoom In," the lens moves from the wide-angle position to the telephoto position in one continuous smooth shot. In a "Zoom Out," the lens moves continuously and smoothly from telephoto to wide-angle position.

A Zoom (In or Out) is the only shot that includes all three basic shots (Long, Medium, and Close) in one single shot. However, Zoom Shots do not conform to our normal way of seeing. They violate the "camera as audience eye" principle. As a result, Zoom Shots call attention to themselves, but they can also create powerful visual effects. For these reasons, they should be used only when appropriate.

For example, the basic Zoom In is an excellent tool to focus on a specific detail in the scene (see photo sequence to the right). Imagine a thief entering the bedroom, looking for a diamond ring. As he searches the room, the camera Zooms In on the ring, revealing its hiding place to the audience. By cutting to a Long Shot of the thief, we've now added considerable interest to the scene. And the quicker the Zoom In, the more emphatic the statement. A quick Zoom, sometimes called a "Snap Zoom," is a visual exclamation point. It's another way of saying "Here it is!!!" The Zoom is especially effective when used sparingly.

A Zoom In can also be used in place of a "cut to" sequence of shots. For example, suppose you were using an Establishing Long Shot of a group of actors followed by a cut to a Close shot of your star. As a substitute, try beginning with the same Long Shot, but this time followed with a slow Zoom In on your star.

Try using the Zoom Out as a dramatic reveal. Start with a Close Shot of your star. Slowly Zoom Out to reveal her in a beautiful lush, green meadow, with a waterfall dramatically cascading in the background. Used here, the Zoom Out first reveals your star, and then her setting.

Example of the use of "Zoom In." →
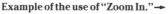

Here are a few tips to produce better Zoom Shots:

1. Use the Zoom sparingly. The most commonly overused effect is the Zoom In. It soon loses its impact and quickly becomes trite.

2. If your camera has a motorized Zoom, use it by all means. But experiment by manually Zooming In and Out at faster and slower speeds than otherwise permitted by the motor control.

3. Preview the Zoom Shot. Look at your starting and ending positions.

4. Use your Zoom lens as many different lenses. Experienced video makers use intermediate lens positions as often as the extreme lens positions. Don't restrict yourself to the widest and narrowest-angle positions. There is life in between!

Depth of Focus

Depth of Focus (also known as "depth of field") refers to the range or distance in front of and behind the subject, that is in focus.

Depth of Focus can be controlled in two ways: First, by the focal length of the lens. A lens in the wide-angle position will produce a picture with a deep range of focus, i.e., virtually everything the lens "sees" will be in focus. A lens in the telephoto position will produce a narrow range of focus, i.e, only the subject itself will be in focus, while the foreground and background will be out of focus. Secondly, Depth of Focus is also

determined by the aperture of the lens. When the diaphragm of the lens is wide open, it will "see" only a narrow range of focus. With the lens stopped down to its smallest aperture, everything, foreground to infinity, will be in focus.

Depth of Focus can be used as a creative tool. Imagine a group of people walking down the sidewalk towards the camera (see photos below). Your job is to shoot the line, but at the same time, feature the woman in front. You can do this with Depth of Focus. Done properly, you'll end up with the people behind your subject out of focus, while your star remains in sharp focus.

Auto-focus cameras (without manual override) make the creative use of Depth of Focus more difficult. But you may still use the technique by shooting your scene in low light, using the telephoto position.

As with all other tools and techniques, experiment and be creative.

Let's Try Some Exercises

1. Find a tall building, monument, statue, or structure. Shoot it in the following ways:

a) A static Long Shot;

b) Start with the Zoom lens fully extended to the telephoto position and slowly Zoom Out to include the entire structure in a Long Shot;

c) Start in the wide-angle position with a Medium to Long Shot of the structure at street level and slowly Tilt up to the top.

Which is more effective as an Establishing Shot?

2. Ask two friends to hold a conversation in front of your camera and shoot them in the following ways:

a) Have them walk in front of the camera and Pan them as they pass;

b) Track them with the camera as they walk and talk;

c) Ask them to start walking towards the camera from a distance and slowly Zoom In, starting with the lens at the extreme telephoto position.

Which shot presents the scene in the most interesting, effective manner?

3. Shoot your house using the techniques described in this chapter. Make each shot *comment* on the subject, rather than just recording the subject. For example, move close in to the house and Pan it to emphasize its size. Track the house from the street to show size in a different way. Go into the living room and, standing in the middle of the room, Pan 360-degrees around the room. Start with a Long Shot of the living room and slowly Zoom In on a family heirloom or treasured possession. See how creative you can be with these silent "narrative flows" as you "comment" on the visualness of your house.

Summary

Now you've learned the basic tools which comprise the language of video: the Long Shot, Medium Shot, Close Shot, the Pan, Tilt, Track, Zoom, and Depth of Focus.

Your next step will be to practice each of these techniques until they become second nature. Your goal will be to have each at your command when the occasion for its use arises.

As with vocabulary, the more words you know, the better stories you can tell. The same is true of your video stories. Learn the tools and use them creatively to tell your tales.

COMPOSITION

6

FIVE SECRETS OF THE PRO'S

Most of us think that the way to photograph people is to put them in front of a camera and start shooting. That's one reason why home videos look amateur when compared to professionally produced television shows. Aside from the obvious difference in budgets and professional actors, there's a difference in the "look" of professionally produced shows. What is that "look," and how can you get it?

The "look" is achieved by following certain rules of composition. By following a few simple rules you, too, can obtain interesting and pleasing images on a regular basis.

In composition, the guiding principle is "balance." Although much about composition is a matter of personal taste, an analysis of pleasing shots reveals that most are *in balance*.

Rule of Thirds

The most important rule of composition is the "Rule of Thirds," which states that an artful balance is achieved by dividing the camera frame into thirds, both horizontally and vertically.

Your frame should look like this:

Not like this:

When it is time to fill the frame with actors and objects, position them so that they are balanced within the frame by placing them in the imaginary sections you've created with the Rule of Thirds. For example, if you're shooting a dialogue between two people, position them like this;

or this;

Such placement creates a sense of balance within the frame and is therefore pleasing to the eye.

Likewise, if you're shooting a park scene, balance the frame this way. Notice how the horizon line bisects the frame exactly one-third of the way up. This one-third/two-thirds division gives the impression of spaciousness.

Adhering to the Rule of Thirds is more effective than shooting the same scene this way.

The Rule of Thirds applies no matter what the elements in your frame. For example, if you're shooting a scene with two trees as the focal point, you'd frame your shot this way:

In the field of creative arts, it is said that rules are made to be broken, and so it is with the Rule of Thirds. But the rule should only be broken in order to achieve a particular visual effect; as for example, to emphasize the distance from the foreground to the church at the top of the hill:

The Rule of Thirds can be broken to achieve a particular visual effect, as shown here.

If you carefully examine the compositional aspects of any television show or movie, you'll soon see just how "standard" is the Rule of Thirds, and how often it is adhered to. And the rule applies equally to the basic shots (Long, Medium, and Close) as it does to Panning, Zooming and Tracking Shots. For example, if you're Panning a man walking down the street, keep him one-third of the way into the frame, with the remaining two-thirds in front of him.

Always have your subject one-third of the way into the frame, with two-thirds in front.

Here, though, you're more interested in giving the impression of him walking into the frame, not out of it, than you are of balance.

Emphasizing Diagonals

Another rule of Composition calls attention to diagonal lines and is called "Diagonal Emphasis." This rule is based on the principle that diagonals are inherently more pleasing to the eye than horizontals or verticals. For example, when shooting a city street scene, it is more pleasing to make this choice;

than this one,

Likewise, shooting a railroad track looks better this way;

than this way.

And remember, the rules of art and composition are made to be broken ...but only for good reason: *to achieve a particular effect.*

Camera Angles

Another rule relates to camera height in relation to the subject. If your subjects are seated, bring the camera down to eye level. Notice that in the Johnny Carson Show, or any talk show where the guests are seated, the camera is positioned at the same height as the seated guests. If the camera were to be positioned at standing height, looking down on the guests, the image created (in most every sense) would not be pleasing. Conversely, if your actors are standing, raise the camera to look them in the eye.

As with the other Rules of Composition, the camera height rule should be broken to achieve a particular visual effect. Shooting up like this emphasizes height:

Shooting down like this reinforces the impression of "small" and tells the story from your subject's point of view:

Creative Focus

Although not a rule of composition, the visual effect of the camera position in relation to a moving subject is important to keep in mind. Objects moving directly toward the camera appear to be traveling slower than objects moving at the same speed traveling across the frame, from side to side. For this reason, it is easier to focus (whether auto or manual) on objects moving toward the camera.

By keeping only your speaker in focus, as shown in the two above photos, you are using Creative Focus.

In the chapter on Expanding the Language, we explained Depth of Focus. Focus can also be used as a compositional tool. In the vast majority of your shots, you will want the subject to be in focus. But interesting visual effects can be created by shooting your subject out of focus. Remember the Dodge City Shoot-Out earlier in the book? Picture the Sheriff and the Villain facing each other in the street. As the Sheriff speaks, the lens is focused on him. When Evil Rance Devlin responds, he comes into sharp focus while the Sheriff goes out of focus; Creative Focus thus emphasizes the speaker. In order to achieve this effect, as you learned in Depth of Focus, the lens aperture will have to be nearly wide open (fl.2, fl.4, fl.8, f2). Otherwise, your Depth of Focus will bring *everything* in the scene into focus.

Framing

When you think about framing a picture, you might think about a picture frame. Framed pictures are more attractive than frameless ones. You can put the same principle to work when composing your video shots. Framing your shots with the elements in a setting can create an extremely pleasing picture. For example, notice in landscape shots how often the director or cameraman will include a few branches of a tree, a flower, the corner of a building, or some other element of the setting at the edge of the frame. Using existing elements to frame your shot not only creates a pleasing picture, but can also add a third dimension, by communicating the distance from the framing object in the foreground to the subject, or to the horizon.

Try experimenting with framing. With a little practice, you'll turn out better looking shots.

Example of a well-framed shot.

Summary

The Rule of Thirds, diagonal emphasis, camera height, camera angle, focus, and framing should be followed in the majority of shooting situations. By doing so, you will achieve video productions which look professional. But break any or all of the rules when you want to produce a startling visual effect.

POINT OF REFERENCE

7

"CROSSING THE LINE"

When shooting a video, it's important to rivet the audience on the story, not the director's techniques. For an audience to be involved in a story, they must see only the story as it unfolds, not the camera's location. To ensure audience attention, you should understand the concept of "Audience Eye" and then stay within the bounds of what that "eye" can see. By following a few guidelines, you'll create videos which unfold in a smooth, seamless, narrative flow, grabbing and holding the audience from beginning to end.

The Audience Eye

Point of Reference and "Audience Eye" are directly related. "Audience Eye" is the intangible element flowing through a series of images which ensures that the audience knows where it is (Point of Reference) in relation to the action on the screen. When the principle of "Audience Eye" is violated, confusion results. For example, we open with a Long Shot of the Sheriff and Evil Rance Devlin facing each other in the street. Devlin is facing right, and the Sheriff is facing left. Cut to a Close Shot of the Sheriff, who is now facing right. What happened? The video maker has reversed his position and shot the Sheriff from the other side without informing the audience. The audience is confused. They don't know if the Sheriff has turned around (and they missed it), or what? Cut to Devlin, facing left. It now appears to the viewer as if Devlin and the Sheriff are back to back, facing in opposite directions. Notice that neither one of them has moved, only the camera has. And this Point of Reference change has totally confused the audience.

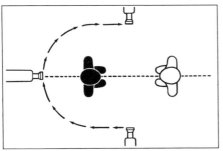

Example of how to cross the "line" correctly using the Long Take.

The Line – And How to Cross It?

How do you avoid confusion? It's easy once you master the principle of the "line." The "line" is an imaginary line. It could be the line created by the direction in which your actor is walking; or, in the case of the Sheriff and the Villain, the line between them; or, the line created by the direction in which the heroine looks as her hero rides his horse off into the sunset. However the "line" is created, it exists in virtually every scene. As such, the "line" provides the audience with a point of reference. Imagine network coverage of a Super Bowl Game, alternately broadcasting from cameras shooting on either side of the 50-yard line. The audience would quickly become confused, not knowing which direction their team was running or why they were periodically running in the wrong direction.

The "line" is not sacred, however, and it can be crossesd without confusing the audience. How?

The *Long Take* is the easy way. Here, the camera crosses the line during the take. In the Dodge City scene, the camera operator might walk around behind the Villain during the take and make his way to the other end of the street with the camera rolling, thereby informing the audience of this change of camera position.

Another solution is the *Intermediate Transition Shot*. Instead of shooting the Sheriff and the Villain first from one side of the street and then immediately from the other side, stop partway and shoot a transition...naturally showing the audience as you make your way across the street.

Summary

The principles of Crossing the Line, Point of Reference and Audience Eye are really nothing more than common sense rules. Once you get into the habit of "seeing" the line, you'll begin to cross it without violating the rules and without causing confusion to your audience. Your goal should be to keep the audience on the story, not on your technique - or your mistakes. But remember, too, that rules are made to be broken. If you want to deliberately shock or confuse the audience, by all means break the rules!

Example of how to cross the "line" using the Intermediate Transition Shot.

SOUND

8

THE OTHER HALF OF VIDEO

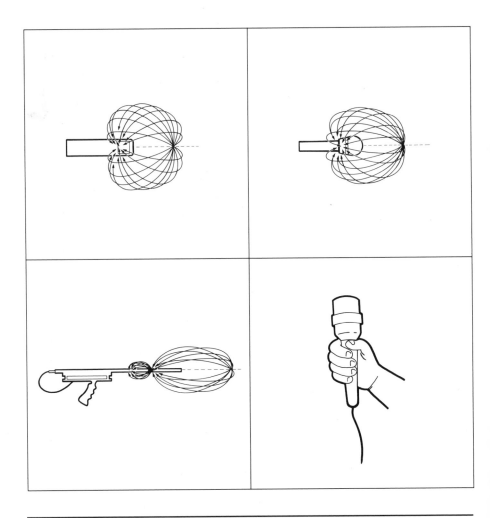

Your camera probably comes equipped with a built-in microphone. This mike is the most convenient to use. However, as you experiment with video productions, you'll want to progress on to one or more external microphones to capture better sound quality.

Video tape not only records visual images, but sound as well. Here's how a section of video tape is constructed:

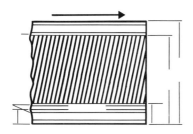

Sound is one of the most important elements of a video production. In addition to the obvious - recording dialogue - you can use sound to create effects such as the crunching of footsteps in the snow; or to create a romantic mood - by playing soft music in the background.

And through use of the *audio dubbing feature* on most VCR's, you can record sound on the audio track only after you've completed the shoot - at the editing stage, for example. This is especially useful if you want to record a voice-over to explain the action on the screen or to re-record the inaudible voice of the speaker.

Since most of your sound recordings will consist of people speaking, let's look at what's involved.

Using the Built-In Microphone

For sheer convenience, most of your shooting will be done with the camera's built-in microphone. Here are a couple of points to keep in mind:

1. Unlike the camera, which can "see" an image up to 50 feet, 100 feet or 200 feet away - and even further with a good telephoto lens - the built-in mike has an extremely limited range. It can only pick up clear sound no more than 15-20 feet away. This may hamper your creative instincts, since a Close Shot or Medium Shot may be inappropriate for the mood you're trying to create. But you are limited, nevertheless, by the built-in mike. It has limited sensitivity - beyond 15-20 feet, the sound is faint and garbled.

2. When using the built-in mike, aim it directly at the speaker. Although built-in mikes are *omni-directional* (they pick up sound from all directions), a direct aim will help ensure that the speaker's voice is recorded properly.

3. Because the built-in mike is omni-directional, you'll have to carefully control all sound emanating from the set - and that means from you and the crew, too. An omni-directional mike will pick up sound from behind the camera, as well as in front of it.

4. Virtually all built-in mikes are equipped with *automatic level control*. This feature "reaches out" and grabs any and every sound, even a low dim hum or low level background noise. Once captured, automatic level control will automatically turn up the recording volume and record these sounds nearly as loud as the featured speakers. That's why it's so crucial to get the proper distance and direction between the mike and the speakers. Remember that the closer you can get the mike to the sound source, the better the sound quality will be on the finished product.

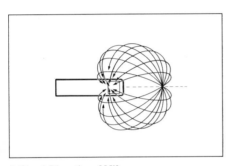

1. Omni-Directional Mike

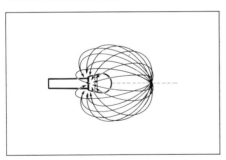

2. Cardoid Mike

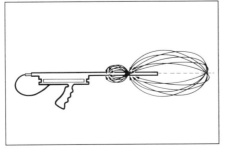

3. Super-Cardoid Mike

Using External Microphones

No matter how much you try, some situations will simply be inappropriate for a built-in mike. To cope, you'll need to know about *external microphones*.

External mikes are available in 3 basic designs: 1) *Omni-Directional;* 2) *Cardoid* (heart-shaped), and 3) *Super-Cardoid* (uni-directional). Each captures all sound within its range. The range of each is pictured to the left.

For video, the Cardoid and Super-Cardoid designs are ideal.

External mikes remove the limitations previously encountered with built-in mikes. But keep in mind that the external mike must be positioned out of the camera's view.

Recording indoors provides some control over extraneous noises that may interfere with the subject. Make certain the mike placement will clearly capture the subject's voice. Recording outdoors will force you into dealing with unwanted sounds such as low flying aircraft, distant traffic, and other extraneous and interfering sounds.

Wind noise can also be disruptive. To avoid the whistling sound of wind, place a wind shield of foam, or made from a handkerchief, over your mike.

External mikes can be supported with a mike stand such as this:

A boom stand like this:

Supported by the speaker - a hand-held mike, especially in man-on-the-street interviews:

Lavalier mikes (also known as personal microphones) can be clipped to the speaker, or to an article of clothing.

If you're using two or more external mikes, you'll need a *mixer.* This handy device allows you to balance the sound coming from both mikes and then feed the single balanced sound signal into the camera.

Sound in the Editing Stage

Using the audio dubbing feature of your VCR you can re-record the sound track when you are editing. This will not affect the video track. The main drawback is that you will erase the original soundtrack. Like a tape recorder or audio cassette recorder, when you record over existing sound, the audio dub automatically erases the previously recorded material on that portion of the tape.

Despite its limitations, post production sound dubbing can enhance your video. Mood music, sound effects, and voice-overs can all be used effectively to enhance and professionalize your production.

Summary

For convenience, use your camera's built-in mike. To get good sound quality, you must record at a distance of no more than 15-20 feet from your speaker. Control the sound on your set, since an omni-directional mike picks up sound from all directions. External mikes allow for greater camera creativity, since you are no longer restricted to 15-20 feet, nor subject to extraneous sounds.

LIGHTING

9

"SHINE IT ON"

The video camera, like its predecessor the film camera, is a mechanical device designed to imitate the human eye. The camera "sees" through a combination of its lens and photosensitive tube or chip, much the same as we see through our eyes. But "seeing," whether through the camera lens or the human eye, requires *illumination* on the subject. (Remember that five-foot stack of gold bars in the pitch black room?)

The principal difference between the eye and the camera lens/tube combination is *sensitivity to light:* The human eye is far more light sensitive than a video camera. Used in this way, "light sensitive" means that the human eye can see objects lit with a bare minimum of light. Cameras, on the other hand, require much higher levels of light in order to "see."

Light Sensitive Tubes and Chips

Video tape can only record images "seen" by the camera, so it's primarily the camera that is responsible for creating the electronic images we shoot. Cameras "see" through the light sensitive tube installed inside. The more sensitive the tube, the better the camera can "see" objects in low light and in extremely bright light. Because of size limitations, however, tubes are being replaced by light sensitive microchips. Chips are smaller and more reliable than tubes, and will not sustain damage if pointed at the sun. But tubes still "see" better at low lights.

Because certain minimum levels of light are required to produce an image on tape, you should have some basic lighting information (and equipment) at your fingertips. Later on, in another book in this series, we'll really get into more sophisticated lighting concepts and equipment. But for right now, we'll stick to the basics.

Minimum Levels of Light

At the start, your most important concern will be to get something on tape which looks good. Every camera has a certain minimum level of light intensity required to produce an image. Read your owner's manual to find your camera's minimum level. You'll probably see something like "20 Lux" or "50 Lux" or "2 footcandles," or some other mumbo-jumbo. What do these numbers mean? We suggest that instead of trying to figure out their meaning, you simply experiment by shooting in various low light situations and see for yourself the images produced. You'll probably find that in order to get an acceptable picture, you're going to need quite a bit of light.

Lighting falls into two major categories - *indoor* and *outdoor*. Indoor light is also known as artificial light. Both categories of light have two characteristics in common.

Shadows

While light illuminates a subject, it also casts shadows. You should "fill" the shadows with additional light, whether shooting indoors or out.

No fill light was used in taking the top photo. The addition of the fill light (second photo) eliminates unwanted shadows.

Shapes

Video is a two-dimensional medium. Therefore, bright light can wash out your subject, making the subject appear flat, dull and uninteresting. Too much light is as much an enemy of good pictures as too little. Arrange your lighting to mold the features of your subject and to help create shapes.

Too much light was used in the third photo, resulting in a "washed out" appearance. By reducing the amount of light, the subject takes shape and becomes more defined.

Indoor Lighting

There are four principal "studio" or indoor lighting techniques you'll need to know about. They are 1) *key lighting,* 2) *fill lighting,* 3) *back lighting,* and 4) *background lighting.* Each performs a different function and is continually used by movie and television lighting directors in Hollywood and in other production centers of the world. When shooting indoors, remember to select the correct *color temperature* position on the camera. Artificial light and natural light cast different colors, and the camera can compensate for this difference.

Key light is usually the main source of illumination for your subject. The key light is normally placed in front of the subject, positioned off to one side, and raised above the subject. Placement off to the side (rather than head-on) tends to "shape" the subject by casting shadows and creating contrast. The key light is a narrow, focused light which, when used in combination with other light sources, highlights and features the subject. If the storyboard calls for a dark, contrasty mood, only the key light will be used.

Usually, however, the key light is balanced by a *fill light.* The fill light is a softer, more diffused light. It "fills in" the shadows produced by the key light. You can experiment with the balance created by these two light sources. Move them around until you get precisely the desired effect. Light and shadow create moods, shapes and contrast. High contrast is harsh, while low contrast is soft. Use lighting to create the mood your story requires.

Illustration of how to set up key lighting.

Photo taken using key lighting.

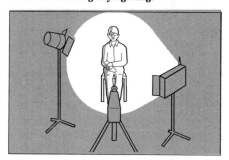

Illustration of how to set up fill lighting.

Photo taken using fill lighting.

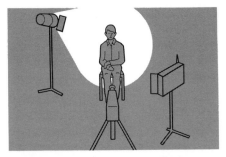

Illustration of how to set up back lighting.

Photo taken using back lighting.

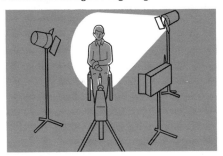

Illustration of how to set up background lighting.

Photo taken using background lighting.

You can also use *window light* as a key or fill light source. Light coming in through the window, because it is low in contrast, is very soft and even; it creates very flattering light.

Back light is a light source placed *behind* the subject. It adds depth and dimension to the scene and makes the subject stand out from the background. Back light provides a certain look of "quality" to the subject. Placement of the back light is important. The source must be positioned high enough so as not to be "seen" by the camera. Otherwise the light will produce flare and wash out the recorded image.

Background light is thrown directly onto the background. The purpose is to bring out the background. As with back light, background light adds a look of quality to your video.

How many light sources do you need to produce a good looking video? You need enough light 1) to see the set, 2) to feature and highlight your subject, and 3) to create the desired mood.

If your storyboard (and wallet) calls for all of the light sources we've just discussed, you'll be using "four-point lighting." Here's a typical set, with a diagram of how all of these lights are employed.

Shooting Outdoors

It is likely that much of your shooting will take place out of doors. You'll be taping sporting events, family outings, school events, summer festivities, and more. What do you need to know about outdoor lighting? Probably the most important things to know are the position, direction, and intensity of the sun in relation to the camera and the subject.

When the sun is out, it casts shadows. But on a cloudy day, the daylight is very even, and low in contrast. Therefore, shooting on cloudy days usually produces pleasing, video images.

In bright sunlight, the biggest lighting problems are shadows and contrast. "Contrast" is the relationship between the brightest bright and the darkest dark in the same scene. Video cameras can only "see" a limited amount of contrast; usually, far less than exists on the average sunny day. Bright light washes out to white, while the dark shadows turn to black. How do you tackle contrast? If you adjust the lens aperture for the brightest bright, the shadows will black out completely

and the camera will see no detail in the shadows - only black. If you adjust for shadows, the brightly lit portions of your subject will burn out, and you'll see only white - with no details. Here's your choice of solutions: 1) use a reflector to fill in (or light up) the shadows, 2) use a high powered mini-lamp (such as a quartz gun) to fill in the shadows, or 3) diffuse the direct sunlight by placing a large sheet or gauze screen between the sun and the subject. All of these solutions reduce the range of contrast between the darks and lights either by lighting the darks or by darkening the lights. If you use a mini-lamp (artificial light), be sure to place a blue filter over it to make it the same color as the sun (which casts a blue-colored light).

At the beginning and end of the day, the sunlight shapes images by its low angle relative to the earth. But be aware that at these times of day, the sun casts a mostly reddish hue. And if on a cloudy day, contrast is too low to create the mood you want, you'll need a mini-lamp to spruce up the resulting flat, undramatic images.

Lighting for Movement

As we've already pointed out, shooting from one camera position can result in a long, boring scene. To create an interesting video, you'll need to move the camera to show the subject from different angles. To do that, you'll need to plan your lighting placements in advance. Place lighting sources so that your subject is well lit from each pre-chosen camera position.

If the subject will be moving during a shot, make certain that all of his or her movements are pre-planned and coordinated with both lighting and camera placements. Nothing can be more disconcerting than watching a brightly lit subject walk into the shadows and stop, while continuing with his monologue.

Summary

Shooting indoors will require some basic lighting equipment - and a tripod, too. You can probably get by with a key light and a fill light. If you shoot indoors during the daytime, window light will suffice as fill light. Make certain you set the camera's color temperature switch to the "indoor" position.

While indoor lighting normally requires that you *create* the lighting and contrast, outdoor lighting requires that you *control* existing contrast. Various "fill light" methods are available for control.

Lighting for movement creates its own special problems. Your lighting plans should take into account periodic change of camera positions, as well as subject movement during a long take.

The goal of all lighting is to create an interesting image with just enough (not too much) contrast.

DIRECTING A VIDEO PRODUCTION

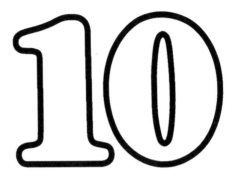

LIGHTS, CAMERA, ACTION!

Every quality video production has a director. He or she must coordinate the efforts of all those involved. In making your own video productions, you will wear many hats: camera operator, person in charge of costumes, props, lights, sound, special effects, editing, and even "gofer" (go-fer this, go-fer that). You'll also be the director.

The Many Jobs Of A Director

A director is responsible for casting the actors, rehearsing and directing them in their roles, choosing locations, sets, determining camera placements and the shots to be made, selecting the lighting moods, sound effects, etc. A director must also decide the order in which the script is to be shot. The order will be decided by taking into consideration the method of editing. If in-camera editing is to be employed, the script will be shot exactly as written. If post production editing equipment facilities are available, the director might select a different shooting order.

How to Show Time And Distance

One of the biggest problems facing a director is how to visually show the passage of time or the distance between places. If your camera has a Fade-In Fade-Out feature, that's ideal to show the passage of time. Fading Out of a scene and into the next scene to show the passage of one day or one week is an excellent method to indicate the passage of time.

Shooting Parallel Action

Intercutting parallel action is an effective way to show events which take place in two different locations. For example, in the Dodge City Shoot-Out, you could cut from a Close-Up of the Sheriff to a Close-Up of his wife with a worried look on her face and then back to the Sheriff. Intercuts can also be used as flashbacks. If the Sheriff were thinking about the last outlaw he faced, you could show the prior gun battle with an intercut flashback shot of the villain.

The following sequence will illustrate how intercutting parallel action works:

Establishing shot - Dodge City.

Cut to a medium shot of our hero.

Cut to a close shot of our hero.

Intercut action - close shot of worried wife.

Intercut flashback shot of the villain.

Cut to a close shot of our hero, ready to draw his gun.

Cut to close shot of our hero's gun firing.

Intercut action - medium shot of the villain, sprawled dead on the street.

Intercut action of wife running to join the sheriff.

Intercut action - wife and our hero embrace.

The Director As Leader

Directing people, more than any other job in production, involves the human element. As such, directing can be one of the most rewarding jobs in video, or it can be one of the most exasperating. The rules for good directing are the same as for any cooperative endeavor. The goal is to have a person, or a group of people, do what you want him or them to do. Here are some general rules to help you reach that goal in each of your productions.

1. Be prepared.

When you first walk into the room or on the set, there is generally an air of anticipation. Everyone is fresh and ready to get to work. The easiest way to dissipate that energy is by not being prepared. If you walk on the set trying to figure out where to begin, where to put the camera, and where to place the actors, everyone's enthusiasm will quickly wither. Instead, have your storyboards sketched out and ready to be used. Study them the night before so you know exactly what you want in that crucial first shot. Be ready to communicate with your actors. Don't fool around with technical details that should have been handled before. The same principles apply to a "happening" event such as a family party or school graduation. Even though no "story" is involved, you'll still be dealing with "actors" whose cooperation in front of the camera will either spell success or disaster for your production.

2. Be specific.

Know what you want and ask for it. Don't say, "Gee, it might look good if you walked in that door." Instead say, "Okay, Bob, here's what I want! Begin the scene here, take seven steps to your right until you're directly behind the couch, then say your line as you look Sharon in the eye." And the same holds true for the technical crew. Don't say, "Gosh, we really could use some fill lights on Sharon's face." That will ensure that everyone stands around looking self-consciously at each other while the task remains undone. Instead, say, "Bruce, pick up that quartz gun, put the blue filter on it, and fill in some light on Sharon's face". Be specific, and be prepared.

3. Be enthusiastic.

You're the leader. The tone of the entire shoot will be set by you. If you treat every problem as if it were a conspiracy to prevent you from finishing, the tone on the set will be dark, troubled and suspicious. If, on the other hand, you make it fun for people to work on your project, if you view problems as opportunities to spur you on to greater creativity, then your actors and crew will be happy and their satisfaction will be reflected in your work. Enthusiasm is catching - and so is the lack of it! Remember, your goal is to create a production you are proud of. However, you must create the production through the cooperation of other people. Be enthusiastic.

4. Get involvement.

Getting everyone involved makes the production a creative, joint effort. Instead of a "you against them" atmosphere, make it "all for one and one for all." Mutual involvement is mutually rewarding. Acknowledge the efforts of those around you. Both during and after the shoot, thank those involved for their contributions to your work. As a rule, most people want to have a good time and a pat on the back for their efforts. This is especially true with an exciting show-biz venture like a video production. If you show them a good time during the shoot and a "thank you" afterwards, they'll be happy to return for more.

Summary

Directing can be one of the most critical functions in a video production. Obtaining the cooperation and assistance of everyone involved should be your goal. If you have little or no experience as a leader, think of a group in which you have participated, where the leader was highly respected. What did that leader do to earn the respect of the group? No doubt, he or she was considerate, courteous, prepared, and enthusiastic. In addition, he or she knew their subject "cold"; they were prepared. And no doubt a good leader can, with courtesy and consideration for the other person, make specific demands and requests. Directing others can be fun. Especially when it is a "win-win," mutually rewarding experience.

EDITING

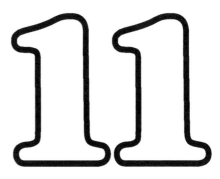

PUTTING IT ALL TOGETHER

In the early days of film-making - around 1900 - editing was unknown. Films were shot in one continuous Long Shot. Early directors simply kept the camera rolling until the film ran out. When all the film magazines had been shot, the exposed films were glued together to form a "movie." Early film producers felt that audiences would not take kindly to editing; they would feel cheated unless they saw every foot of film.

Then, innovators Edwin S. Porter and D.W. Griffith introduced editing to the budding film industry. The concept was simple: View all of the available footage, select only the most appropriate scenes, and reassemble them into an entirely new sequence to produce a unified, concisely told story.

Editing can be done either during or after the shoot. Editing during the shoot requires some pre-planning. Post production editing, while it may save some pre-production time during the planning stages, will require hours of tedious editing time after the shoot. Furthermore, post production editing requires additional equipment: at minimum, a second VCR . . . preferably, a second VCR and an editing controller. Therefore, you are strongly urged to spend time in the planning stages by preparing a story outline, storyboard and script. Pre-production planning will not only save you hours of post production editing time, but will make the shoot more fun and produce a better video story.

Editing during the shoot requires editing-in-the-camera. In other words, you'll only be shooting the scenes that will be included in the finished product. You can accomplish in-camera editing either by using the camera's Pause Control Switch or through the use of the "Long Creative Take."

Pause Control
For In-Camera Editing

Editing in-camera requires that you start and stop the tape as each scene is shot. The important thing is to start and stop the tape smoothly . . . without excessive frame roll. Frame roll is caused by the motor start-up time in the VCR; it takes a fraction of a second for the VCR motor to start winding after the Play/Record button is depressed, thereby causing a delay in recording. The "pause" feature was designed to stop the tape, yet keep the motor running.

To avoid excessive frame roll, you'll be using the Pause Control Switch for in-camera editing. Virtually every camera comes equipped with a Remote Pause Control Switch, which allows you to control taping directly from the camera. Shooting then simply requires that you depress the camera's Pause Control, tape the scene, depress the Pause Control to stop taping, set up and tape the next scene, and repeat the process until you have completed the production.

And while you're moving the camera from place to place, shooting scene after scene, remember the basics: the Long Shot, Medium Shot, and Close Shot. Plan scenes as visual sentences, using all the tools of the video language. Each scene should flow into the next; and each scene should follow-on from the last.

Continuity

Every motion picture and television production has a person in charge of continuity. Continuity ensures that the set, props, costumes, etc., remain exactly the same in every shot, even if the shoot stretches over six months. For example, if the hero has a water glass filled with cola and ice cubes, the glass must be there for every shot in that scene. If the heroine is wearing a cameo on her red blouse, the cameo must be in place everytime she wears the red blouse.

As you plan your shots, keep continuity in mind. Be aware of what's included in each scene; what the actors are wearing, positioning of the furniture, details such as flowers, vases, pictures on the wall, etc. If there's a lot to remember, take a Polaroid shot of the set-up, using it to refresh your memory when you resume shooting.

Continuity is only important when it's overlooked. And it's amazing how quickly an audience will zero-in on scenes which lack continuity. Time spent on detail will pay off in audience attention to your story, not your mistakes.

The Long Take

As an alternative to in-camera editing, try the Long Take. It solves many shooting problems and is easier than in-camera editing. You don't have to start and stop the tape or continually change camera positions. But Long Takes can result in boring scenes if not set-up with care. The object is to achieve a variety of visual images within the Long Take. A creatively staged Long Take should combine the Long Shot, Medium Shot, and Close Shot, and perhaps even Panning or Tracking.

The sequence at the right shows how to set up the shot in a Long Take. Imagine a sinister-looking man enters a living room, approaches the couch, lifts up the middle cushion, hides a book under it, and quickly departs through a different door. If this were staged in a static Long Take, it would be tedious. By using a little imagination, it's possible to stage the action in such a way so as to establish the scene (Long Shot), reveal the face of the man (Close Shot), show him hiding the book - the key element of the scene (Medium Shot), and quickly departing (Long Shot).

All the rules of Panning apply here. It's important to plan the shot, run through it several times, and position yourself to retain your balance throughout the entire shot.

Many of the great film and television directors began as editors. Editing requires that you recognize what's essential to your story and discard the rest. As you gain experience with your camera and discover its possibilities - and limitations - you'll discover that creative editing is one of your most important skills.

Post Production Editing

If you're anything like most new camera owners, you'll begin video-making using in-camera editing techniques. But after a few months of shooting, you will probably have acquired hours of recorded material... some (or much) of it unwanted. What do you do? Don't cut up the tapes and try to glue together all the scenes you want to keep. Do get a second VCR.

Editing Equipment

The bare minimum required for post production editing is a second VCR. Your portable VCR then becomes the replay machine, while the new VCR (portable or tabletop) becomes the editing machine. The concept of editing using two machines is simplicity itself: As you replay the original (master) tape, you record from it only those scenes you want to keep onto the new tape in the editing VCR. The newly recorded tape becomes your edited master. However, while the concept of copy-editing is simple, technical problems abound. Flashes and frame rolls sabotage attempts at clean cuts; visual "noise" pocks the screen with white static marks; audio tracks fail to match from scene to scene; continuity is lacking from scene to scene, etc.

Some of these are equipment problems, while others result from the shooting sequence. Technical problems can be solved by getting the right equipment. Your second VCR should come equipped with a very accurate

Pause Control - at least; or, better still, a purpose-built Edit Control. And, wallet permitting, buy a dedicated, stand-alone editing controller. It allows central control of both the replay VCR and edit VCR by synching them together.

Once you've got the equipment, you'll want to get down to the business of editing. But before you do, let's again examine how a piece of video tape is constructed:

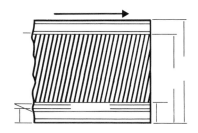

The audio and video tracks contain their respective signals, while the control track synchronizes tape speed with the VCR playback head to assure a stable picture on replay.

"Assembly" is the most basic form of editing. Here, scenes from the master tape are copied or reassembled onto the edit master. The edit VCR is left in the Pause mode, while the replay VCR replays the master tape. As the master tape replays and you come across the scenes you want to keep, you record them on the edit VCR by starting and stopping it via the Pause Control.

"Insert Editing" is more difficult and requires sophisticated equipment. The object is to insert onto an existing previously recorded tape.

When editing video tape, be aware of "generation loss." Each time you copy material from one tape to another, the copy tape is one generation away from its predecessor. With each generation, a loss of visual and audio quality results. The quality loss from generation copying should be borne in mind both when editing and when making copies for friends and relatives.

If you don't have editing equipment readily available, look in your local yellow pages for a TV studio or editing house - call and see if you can rent time there. You'll be surprised how many professional editing studios will gladly rent you time in their facilities . . . and even assist you.

Summary

Editing is most easily accomplished in-the-camera, during a shoot. To produce a well-edited, interesting and entertaining video production, you must pre-plan. Prepare a story outline, storyboard and a script that you, your cast and your crew will follow - even if *you're* performing all three functions. Shooting without a storyboard and scripts is much like driving your car without a destination in mind or a road map by your side . . . you get nowhere!

As you become more experienced, you may want to acquire equipment which will permit post production editing. With a second VCR, you'll be ready to perform assembly editing, and with an editing controller, you can do insert editing. With these sophisticated tools, and some practice, you'll soon be producing professional looking videos. But be aware of generation loss through copying. Consider the use of outside editing facilities if they are available in your area.

PLANNING YOUR OWN VIDEO PRODUCTION

PREPARE TO GET THE BEST

An old proverb states "plan your work and then work your plan." This applies equally to planning a video production. Whether you're shooting a simple, one-camera family picnic or a complex two-camera little league game, *advance planning* is the key to a successful production.

As a video-maker, your productions will fall into two broad categories. For the most part, you'll be shooting events that just happen - "happenings." Happenings include everything from weddings to birthday parties to little league games to baby's first steps to high school graduations, and so on.

You may also be shooting staged events. These could include a planned sales or product presentation for your business, a rock music video performed by a local group, a "TV show" created by you, a short documentary shot for your local public access cable channel, and so on. Although successful and entertaining video requires adherence to a very few, simple rules, it does require planning. How you plan for happenings may differ from planning for staged events - but both shoots require advance planning.

Every profession has its planning tools. For example, architects use blueprints. As a video producer, you'll need to use the tools of your new trade. What are these tools? They are 1) *a story outline,* 2) *a script,* and 3) *a storyboard.*

The top photo (wedding) is an example of a "happening," while the business meeting shown in the lower shot is a planned or "staged" event.

Story Outline

A story outline is simply that - a summary of the story or project, consisting of a list of its most important points. Once you have selected the subject of your production (family picnic, little league game, school graduation, wedding, 25th anniversary party, "talk show" interview, etc.), you should prepare a basic outline. Right from the start, take into account the equipment and personnel you'll have available when you shoot the production.

The outline summarizes the "what, when, why, where and how" of every production. A story outline should answer these questions: What is the main purpose of the video? Who is the audience? How will you begin? How will you tell the story? How will you end? What is the length? For "happenings," all you'll need in the way of advance planning is an outline. It will serve as the basis for the order of shots. But for "staged" productions, such as the "Talk Show" presented later in this book, you'll need a script and a storyboard in order to best control the shoot and the results.

Here is a story outline of the Watsons' family picnic.

The action begins at home, in the kitchen.

The principal characters - Mom, Sis, and Dad - are seen busily making sandwiches and loading the car with all the fixin's and goodies.

On the way to the park to meet the rest of the gang, shoot some familiar landmarks.

On arrival at the park, get out of the car first to shoot Dad and Mom unloading the picnic-baskets and carrying them to the party that's already in progress (Mom is always late!).

As the day progresses, shoot all the events.

Lunch: Be sure to show Tom wolfing down his usual quota of eight sandwiches. Be kind, and don't tape Sis talking with a mouthful of food.

The Baseball Game: Be sure and get a Close-Up of Gus in the funny hat he always wears. Be alert for a fast-breaking fly ball off Elmer's bat. Pick two good camera positions and alternate between them. Be sure to get a good shot of Dad snoring away in the stands, unsuccessfully trying to stay awake for the game.

The Sack Race: Little Billy is real fast at this one. Try to stay with him as you Track down the course.

Gramps and Aunt Martha solving the world's problems: Get a Long Shot of them talking under the old oak tree. Come in closer to get a Medium Shot and to record what Gramps' humorous response is to Aunt Martha's jibes. Zoom in to a Close Shot of Gramps' face to reveal his sparkling eyes and characater-lined face.

Close with a Long Shot of the sun setting over Bear Creek Lake, and slowly Zoom in to a Close Shot of the setting sun.

The video should be approximately 1/2 hour of viewing time.

The picnic party outline was based on the video-maker's knowledge of all the characters. However, you can still make a story outline even when you don't know the people involved. For example, for a high school graduation, you'll still have to plan how to open, the sequence of shots which will tell the story, and how you plan to close. Keep in mind all of your "tools," and plan each production by utilizing each "tool" to its best effect.

How to Create a Script

Using your outline as a guide, prepare a simple script. A script is the "story" blueprint, while a storyboard is the "picture" blueprint of your production. Remember, before you can start shooting, you must decide what you're going to shoot, how, and in what order.

A script is made up of three basic parts: 1) *dialogue,* 2) *stage directions,* and 3) *a short description of the basic shots.* By creating a simple script for your productions, you'll be doing exactly what every great Hollywood director does for his own productions.

In its simplified form, the *dialogue* will be double-spaced and indented 10 spaces from both the left and right margins. *Stage directions,* on the other hand, are single-spaced and not indented. They run to the margins and are typed in all capital letters. Each shot is consecutively numbered and named in capital letters.

Remember the gun battle at Dodge City? Here's how it looks in a story outline followed by a simple script.

Dodge City Story Outline

The story is set in the old West town of Dodge City. It illustrates the triumph of good over evil.

The action takes place at high noon, on Main Street.

The principal characters, Sheriff Jim Kincaid and Evil Rance Devlin, will be acting a six-gun shoot-out.

The finished production will have a running time of approximately ten minutes.

The principal characters will be dressed in cowboy outfits, complete with cowboy hats and boots.

In addition to the principal characters, five or six costumed extras are required to play the townspeople.

Props will include four holstered six-guns, a 5-point "Sheriff's" star, and an old time, pendulum clock.

Technical equipment will include one video camera, one portable video recorder, one television monitor, two portable battery packs, one tripod, and one portable fill light or reflector.

Technical personnel will include camera man/director, a costume person, an assistant director and a lighting/continuity assistant. The extras will double as technical crew.

Dodge City Script

1. LONG SHOT — EXTERIOR, MAIN STREET, DODGE CITY
WE SEE A HOT, DUSTY WESTERN STREET. TWO MEN FACE EACH OTHER. THEY
ARE NOW SOME DISTANCE APART.

2. FULL SHOT — SHERIFF JIM KINCAID
JIM IS WEARING A WHITE HAT. HE HAS A GRIM EXPRESSION ON HIS FACE, AND
A SHINY 5-POINT STAR ON HIS LAPEL.

3. FULL SHOT — EVIL RANCE DEVLIN
COMING TOWARD THE SHERIFF IS EVIL RANCE DEVLIN, DRESSED ALL IN
BLACK. HE IS CARRYING SIX-GUNS THAT ARE ALMOST IDENTICAL TO THOSE
THE SHERIFF HAS. RANCE LOOKS TO HIS LEFT.

4. INSERT CLOSE UP — A CLOCK FACE
WE SEE IT'S HIGH NOON.

5. CLOSE UP — KINCAID'S FACE
HE IS ALSO LOOKING AT THE CLOCK. HE TURNS AND LOOKS THE OPPOSITE
WAY AT HIS DEPUTY, WHO HAS ENTERED THE FRAME AS THE CAMERA PULLS
BACK SLIGHTLY.

DEPUTY

It's time.

SHERIFF

I know.

DEPUTY

Sure you don't want some help?

SHERIFF

This is my battle. I've got to face him alone.

6. LONG SHOT — MAIN STREET, DODGE CITY
WE RETURN TO THE FIRST SHOT AS WE SEE THE MEN START TO STRIDE TO-
WARDS EACH OTHER.

7. TRACKING MEDIUM SHOT — SHERIFF KINCAID
THE CAMERA TRAVELS WITH THE SHERIFF AS HE STRIDES TOWARD THE
ENEMY.

SHERIFF

This is it for you, Devlin. I'm taking care of you once and for all.

8. TRACKING MEDIUM SHOT — EVIL RANCE DEVLIN
FROM THE OTHER DIRECTION COMES RANCE DEVLIN, WITH A SNARL ON HIS
LIPS.

RANCE

We'll just see about that, Sheriff.

9. CLOSE UP — DEVLIN'S GUNS
WE SEE DEVLIN FINGERING HIS PEARL-HANDLED REVOLVER.

10. LONG SHOT — MAIN STREET, DODGE CITY
ONCE AGAIN WE SEE THE SHERIFF AND THE VILLAIN WALKING TOWARD ONE
ANOTHER. FINALLY, WHEN THEY ARE ABOUT 10 PACES FROM EACH OTHER,
THEY STOP.

11. CLOSE UP — DEVLIN'S FACE
UNSMILING, STERN.

12. CLOSE UP — SHERIFF'S FACE
EQUALLY STERN.

SHERIFF

Draw.

13. CLOSE UP — DEVLIN'S HAND
DEVLIN PULLS HIS GUN OUT OF HIS HOLSTER.

14. CLOSE UP — SHERIFF'S HAND
THE SHERIFF PULLS HIS GUN OUT OF HIS HOLSTER. WE SEE HIM ACTUALLY
SQUEEZE OFF 3 BULLETS.

15. LONG SHOT — MAIN STREET
BOTH FIGURES STAND FOR A SPLIT SECOND, THEN DEVLIN FINALLY FALLS
OVER.

16. CLOSE SHOT — SHERIFF'S FACE
THE STERN VISAGE BREAKS INTO A SMALL TIGHT SMILE. HE BLOWS THE
SMOKE FROM HIS GUN BARREL.

17. LONG SHOT — MAIN STREET, DODGE CITY
WE SEE THE SHERIFF TURN AND WALK AWAY. AS HE WALKS AWAY, THE
TOWNSPEOPLE COME OUT AND EXAMINE THE BODY OF THE DECEASED VIL-
LAIN. JUST AS THE SHERIFF TURNS THE CORNER AND DISAPPEARS, WE . . .

FADE OUT

This system of scripting can be used to describe just about any event or dialogue you might think of. The numbering system allows for easy indexing and organizing. If you are using the in-camera method of editing, you will shoot the story in its natural order. However, if you are planning to edit after the shoot (post production editing), you can rearrange the shooting order. For example, in Hollywood, television producers often shoot scenes out of sequence for the sake of time-saving convenience and economy. If you are shooting the Dodge City example, you might order shots 1, 6, 10, 15, and 17 all to be taped from the same camera position, at the same time. They would then be reassembled with all the other shots at the post production editing session.

How to Make a Storyboard

When you build a house, you need to follow a detailed blueprint. Building a house is not just a matter of randomly hammering nails into lumber and "trying to be creative." "Building" a video story utilizes the same principles. Instead of a blueprint, you'll be making, and then using a storyboard.

A *storyboard* is a visual illustration, or pictorial guide, of the production, much like the frames of a comic book.

Why is a storyboard important? Primarily because it provides a high degree of control over the production. It saves time, money, energy, frazzled nerves, and hot tempers. One hour invested in making a storyboard could save five hours, and more, of wasted production time. And, in addition to a faster, smoother shoot, the finished product will undoubtedly be superior. In truth, a storyboard - even a simple one - is virtually indispensable for almost any production. Steve Speilberg storyboarded every single frame of "Raiders of the Lost Ark" so that he could concentrate on the actors and the set, instead of fiddling around with camera placement and wasting time deciding about the next shot.

If storyboarding sounds complicated, don't worry. It's really easy . . . and fun! If you can draw, that's fine. But stick figures will suffice. Just remember that a picture (even of stick figures) is worth a thousand words.

A storyboard *frame* is simply a picture of what you want in a particular shot. Dialogue and sound effects are listed below each picture frame. Here's a storyboard of the Dodge City shoot-out, using all the parts of speech: the Long Shot, Medium Shot, Close Shot, the Pan, Zoom, Tilt, Track, and Creative Focus.

Dodge City Storyboard

1. LONG SHOT EXTERIOR, MAIN STREET, DODGE CITY WE SEE A HOT, DUSTY WESTERN STREET. TWO MEN FACE EACH OTHER. THEY ARE NOW SOME DISTANCE APART.

2. FULL SHOT SHERIFF JIM KINCAID
JIM IS WEARING A WHITE HAT. HE HAS A GRIM EXPRESSION ON HIS FACE, AND A SHINY 5-POINT STAR ON HIS LAPEL.

3. FULL SHOT — EVIL RANCE DEVLIN
COMING TOWARD THE SHERIFF IS EVIL RANCE DEVLIN, DRESSED ALL IN BLACK. HE IS CARRYING SIX-GUNS THAT ARE ALMOST IDENTICAL TO THOSE THE SHERIFF HAS. RANCE LOOKS TO HIS LEFT.

4. INSERT CLOSE UP A CLOCK FACE
WE SEE IT'S HIGH NOON.

5. CLOSE UP — KINCAID'S FACE
HE IS ALSO LOOKING AT THE CLOCK. HE TURNS AND LOOKS THE OPPOSITE WAY AT HIS DEPUTY, WHO HAS ENTERED THE FRAME AS THE CAMERA PULLS BACK SLIGHTLY.
DEPUTY: It's time.
SHERIFF: I know.
DEPUTY: Sure you don't want some help?
SHERIFF: This is my battle. I've got to face him alone.

6. LONG SHOT — MAIN STREET, DODGE CITY
WE RETURN TO THE FIRST SHOT AS WE SEE THE MEN START TO STRIDE TOWARDS EACH OTHER.

7. TRACKING MEDIUM SHOT — SHERIFF KINCAID
THE CAMERA TRAVELS WITH THE SHERIFF AS HE STRIDES TOWARD THE ENEMY.
SHERIFF: This is it for you, Devlin. I'm taking care of you once and for all.

8. TRACKING MEDIUM SHOT — EVIL RANCE DEVLIN
FROM THE OTHER DIRECTION COMES RANCE DEVLIN, WITH A SNARL ON HIS LIPS.
RANCE: We'll just see about that, Sheriff.

9. CLOSE UP — DEVLIN'S GUNS
WE SEE DEVLIN FINGERING HIS PEARL-HANDLED REVOLVER.

(continued next page)

10. LONG SHOT — MAIN STREET, DODGE CITY
ONCE AGAIN WE SEE THE SHERIFF AND THE VILLAIN WALKING TOWARD ONE ANOTHER. FINALLY, WHEN THEY ARE ABOUT 10 PACES FROM EACH OTHER, THEY STOP.

11. CLOSE UP — DEVLIN'S FACE
UNSMILING, STERN.

12. CLOSE UP — SHERIFF'S FACE
EQUALLY STERN.
SHERIFF: Draw.

13. CLOSE UP — DEVLIN'S HAND
DEVLIN PULLS HIS GUN OUT OF HIS HOLSTER.

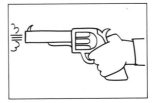

14. CLOSE UP — SHERIFF'S HAND
THE SHERIFF PULLS HIS GUN OUT OF HIS HOLSTER. WE SEE HIM ACTUALLY SQUEEZE OFF 3 BULLETS.

15. LONG SHOT — MAIN STREET
BOTH FIGURES STAND FOR A SPLIT SECOND, THEN DEVLIN FINALLY FALLS OVER.

16. CLOSE SHOT — SHERIFF'S FACE
THE STERN VISAGE BREAKS INTO A SMALL TIGHT SMILE. HE BLOWS THE SMOKE FROM HIS GUN BARREL.

17. LONG SHOT — MAIN STREET, DODGE CITY
WE SEE THE SHERIFF TURN AND WALK AWAY. AS HE WALKS AWAY, THE TOWNS-PEOPLE COME OUT AND EX-AMINE THE BODY OF THE DECEASED VILLAIN. JUST AS THE SHERIFF TURNS THE CORNER AND DISAPPEARS, WE...
FADE OUT

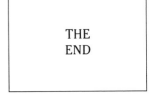

THE
END

Storyboarding can be the most creative part of your video projects. It's also at this stage that you decide where to place the camera, what to show the audience, and the sequence of scenes. The more detail you storyboard, the more self-assured you'll be on the set and the more fun you'll have experimenting with variations on your creative ideas.

Titles and Credits

Titles and credits are known as graphics. They are a good way to open and close your videos. Graphics can also be used to illustrate or explain the speaker's topic. For example, if you're making a video on geography, you could use a Close Shot of a map to graphically illustrate your speaker's point.

If your camera has a character generator, you can use it to superimpose titles and credits over the video picture. If your camera does not have this feature, you'll have to make up titles by using rub-on letters on a piece of cardboard or paper and then shoot them propped up against a steady support. Or, you could hand letter a title card and shoot it the same way. Shoot the title cards using a Close Shot to fill up the entire frame.

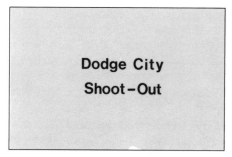

Title made with rub-on letters.

Hand-lettered title.

Summary

Advance planning is the key to a successful video production. Planning begins with a story outline. The outline summarizes the what, when, where, why, and how of your production. From the outline, you can prepare a simple script. A script has three basic parts: 1) dialogue, 2) stage directions, and 3) a short description of the basic shots. Finally, make a storyboard. The storyboard will serve as a visual guide to everyone involved in the production.

LET'S START THE FUN

"THE TALK SHOW"

SCRIPT FOR 'THE JONES FAMILY VIDEO'

1. LONG SHOT — LIVING ROOM OF THE JONES FAMILY
IN THIS LIVING ROOM, THERE IS A LONG COUCH ANGLED TOWARD A MATCHING SINGLE CHAIR. AN ELDERLY MAN SITS ON THE COUCH HOLDING A FAMILY ALBUM OF PHOTOGRAPHS. IN THE CHAIR IS A YOUNGER MAN, HIS SON.

RALPH

Hi, this is Ralph Jones, and welcome to another chapter of the Jones

Family Album.

2. MEDIUM SHOT — ANGLE ON OLDER MAN
NOW RALPH IS IN PROFILE, AND THE GUEST, STANLEY JONES, IS FULL FACE TO THE CAMERA.

RALPH

Today, it's my great pleasure and honor to have my father, Stanley

Jones, on the show. Stanley was born in this very city many years ago,

and he's brought along his own family photo album to show us some

snapshots of his early years.

3. SLOW ZOOM — ZOOM IN ON FAMILY ALBUM TILL IT BECOMES A CLOSE UP.

STANLEY

This city has sure changed a lot since I was a boy.

HE OPENS THE ALBUM TO A SPECIFIC (PRE-PLANNED) PHOTO.

See this empty lot here? We used to play stickball in this lot. Now there's

a shopping mall there.

THE CAMERA PANS AS HE POINTS TO ANOTHER PHOTO.

And here's my brother, your uncle, standing in a bean field. That bean

field is where the new city hall was built in 1966.

Now that you have the basic rules for creating a video, let's put them to work and actually produce your own video. To begin, we've selected the "talk show" format. A talk show is one of the most popular television show formats. The "Tonight Show" with Johnny Carson has been on the air for over 20 years. That's a tribute to Johnny Carson and the network. However, most of all, it's a tribute to the talk show format. Perhaps that's because of its simplicity - human beings sitting down and informally talking to each other and to the audience. The "talk show" is a perfect vehicle to focus attention on the unique personality of each guest. It provides the viewer with a personal in-depth look at the guest. And from the guest's stand-point, it is an easy show to do. Rehearsal is minimal and no lines or script need be memorized. All that's required of a guest is simply "to be yourself."

If your guest is camera shy, you should volunteer to go first. He or she will see how easy it is. And you'll understand what he or she will be going through. To start with, pick the easiest person to interview. That will set an example for all the other participants. Have the host rehearse questions and topics with each guest. This will help relax the guest and will alert you and your crew as to what may be expected.

Once you get started, split up the interview into parts. Periodically starting and stopping gives the host and guest a break and permits the camera operator to change positions and shoot from different angles. Remember D.W. Griffith? He unbolted the camera from its fixed position and moved it around to shoot from different, interesting angles. To begin and end each sequence smoothly, develop a few signals between camera operator, host, and guest, so that each participant knows when taping will begin and end.

Keep in mind that most people are shocked when they see themselves on television for the first time. Each of us has a self-image that may or may not square with what we see on TV. If you see this reaction, reassure the person that he or she looks fine.

The following storyboard sequence is a guide for creating your own talk show. You'll see the camera position, the set, the lighting, and some sample dialogue. There's even a "commercial" in the middle so that other family members can appear before the camera.

Making videos is a fun family activity. In this "talk show" script, three family members are involved. You can use other family members to assist and work as the technical crew. What follows is a sample script. You can create your own scripts, using your own family members as guests. Naturally, each of your guests will relate his or her own story. So use the sample script as a guide.

The following talk show has Mr. Stanley Jones as its principal guest. Stanley's son, Ralph Jones, is the host. Ralph's son, Timmy Jones, delivers his own "commercial." The show is produced in Ralph's living room. Timmy's commercial is shot in front of the Jones' family house. You may use either artificial lighting or adequate window lighting for the interview shots. In his interview, Stanley will be asked to reminisce about his early years. In addition to being a fun project, Ralph intends to keep Stanley's interview as a permanent collection in his Jones' "family album." Ralph's video family album will become a modern-day prized family collection much like snap-shot albums used to be in pre-video days. The "talk show" format is an elegant, yet simple method for producing a video family album.

Let's set up the talk show in script form. Remember, a script is just a blueprint to assist you in creating your video. The talk show is something of a special case in scripting, because, by its very nature, it is impossible to plan what is going to be said. What you can plan is the way in which your guests are visually presented. You'll be doing that later with a storyboard.

But first, a couple of guidelines. When framing your host and guest in a Long Shot, be sure to keep them both in the shot. This is to make sure the audience understands that the guest is talking to another person, and not just to a blank wall. A talk show is an excellent place for the occasional use of the Zoom lens. Since you're never quite sure what will happen next, you won't have time to change camera angles or camera placement when presented with dramatic or humorous moments. If a guest reminisces about his childhood, and says something that is exceptionally moving and personal, that might be an appropriate time to Zoom in on his face, to emphasize the importance of the moment and "show" his emotions.

The key to producing an interesting, fast moving and good looking family talk show is *planning*. Yes, even with a program like this where a premium is placed on spontaneity, planning is essential. The host and guest should predetermine what questions the host is going to ask so the guest can make his answers as succinct and interesting as possible. If there are any photographs or charts that need to be displayed, the presentation should be rehearsed to facilitate a smooth and interesting program.

Let's set up a talk show in script form. For the purpose of our sample script, we'll actually include the dialogue as it might develop, to help you see just how many possibilities there are in staging a show like this.

SCRIPT FOR 'THE JONES FAMILY VIDEO'

1. LONG SHOT — LIVING ROOM OF THE JONES FAMILY
IN THIS LIVING ROOM, THERE IS A LONG COUCH ANGLED TOWARD A MATCH-
ING SINGLE CHAIR. AN ELDERLY MAN SITS ON THE COUCH HOLDING A FAMI-
LY ALBUM OF PHOTOGRAPHS. IN THE CHAIR IS A YOUNGER MAN, HIS SON.

RALPH

Hi, this is Ralph Jones, and welcome to another chapter of the Jones

Family Album.

2. MEDIUM SHOT — ANGLE ON OLDER MAN
NOW RALPH IS IN PROFILE, AND THE GUEST, STANLEY JONES, IS FULL FACE
TO THE CAMERA.

RALPH

Today, it's my great pleasure and honor to have my father, Stanley

Jones, on the show. Stanley was born in this very city many years ago,

and he's brought along his own family photo album to show us some

snapshots of his early years.

3. SLOW ZOOM — ZOOM IN ON FAMILY ALBUM TILL IT BECOMES A CLOSE
UP.

STANLEY

This city has sure changed a lot since I was a boy.

HE OPENS THE ALBUM TO A SPECIFIC (PRE-PLANNED) PHOTO.

See this empty lot here? We used to play stickball in this lot. Now there's

a shopping mall there.

THE CAMERA PANS AS HE POINTS TO ANOTHER PHOTO.

And here's my brother, your uncle, standing in a bean field. That bean

field is where the new city hall was built in 1966.

4. LONG SHOT — JONES FAMILY LIVING ROOM
ONCE AGAIN WE SEE BOTH RALPH AND STANLEY.

RALPH

What was the city like when you first moved here, in . . .

STANLEY

. . . 1947. I'll never forget it as long as I live.

CAMERA SLOWLY ZOOMS IN ON A CLOSE SHOT OF STANLEY'S FACE.

When we left our home back East, it had been snowing, and it was 5 below zero. When we got off the train here, it was 77 degrees, the sun was shining, and the whole place smelled like orange blossoms.

CAMERA PULLS BACK INTO A MEDIUM SHOT WITH RALPH AND STANLEY.

RALPH

Dad, I'd really like to see some more photos from the family album, but first, another member of our family has a short commercial message.

CUT TO:

5. MEDIUM SHOT — EXTERIOR. BOY STANDING NEXT TO LAWNMOWER.
ELEVEN YEAR OLD TIMMY JONES ADDRESSES THE CAMERA.

TIMMY

Hi, this is Timmy Jones. This summer my parents said I could have a bicycle if I could make $50 mowing lawns, so I'd like to mow your lawn. I'm a hard worker, I'll bring my own mower over, and I'll do your whole yard for $2.00, or just a dollar for the front yard only.

CAMERA SLOWLY ZOOMS IN ON TIMMY'S FACE.

Just come by my house and say you want Timmy Jones to mow your lawn. Thanks a lot.

CUT TO:

6. LONG SHOT — JONES FAMILY LIVING ROOM
A RETURN TO THE SAME SET UP AS THE BEGINNING.

> RALPH

> I understand you have a photograph of me when I was 8 years old, in front of Finley Park.

7. MEDIUM SHOT — ANGLE ON OLDER MAN. ONCE AGAIN, WE SEE STANLEY OVER RALPH'S SHOULDER. HE OPENS HIS VIDEO ALBUM.

> STANLEY

> Yep, it's right here.

THE CAMERA ZOOMS IN ON A CLOSE SHOT OF A PHOTO IN THE ALBUM.

> That was where the old minor league team, the Bulldogs, used to play their games. In fact, the day that I took this photograph, you got hit in the head with a foul ball.

> RALPH

> I remember that!

THE CAMERA PULLS BACK TO REVEAL STANLEY ONCE AGAIN IN A MEDIUM SHOT.

> STANLEY

> And after the game, we went down and had the ball autographed.

8. A LONG SHOT — COUCH IN LIVING ROOM

> RALPH

> I still have that baseball, right here (holds up ball). Well, that concludes this edition of the Jones Family Album. Next time, my guest will be Dorothy Jones, Stanley's wife and my mom, who will tell us all about her experiences as a Red Cross Nurse during World War II. Good bye!

> THE END.

This is the basic script for the talk show. Always begin a segment with a Long Shot, to orient the audience. Then plan the rest of the show to emphasize the entertainment and historical value of what is being presented. Notice how smoothly the photographs were integrated into the show. Each topic that Ralph brought up was planned in advance with Stanley to avoid pauses, fidgets and confusion. Each change to a different angle was also plotted in advance, to give the audience a variety of images.

The key to all this is *planning*. For an initial effort, keep your show under ten minutes, and plan it out with both a script and storyboards. Remember, stick figures are fine.

Below and on the next page, we show how that talk could be planned on storyboards.

Summary

These are the tools you need to use your video camera in new and creative ways. Remember, the most important tool you have is not your camera, or your recorder, or your monitor. It's your *imagination*. Try different things. Experiment. Imitate what you see professional television directors do. Learn the rules, and then don't be afraid to break them. Have fun. You're on your way!

STORYBOARD OF THE TALK SHOW

1. LONG SHOT LIVING ROOM OF THE JONES FAMILY
IN THIS LIVING ROOM, THERE IS A LONG COUCH ANGLED TOWARD A MATCHING SINGLE CHAIR. AN ELDERLY MAN SITS ON THE COUCH HOLDING A FAMILY ALBUM OF PHOTOGRAPHS. IN THE CHAIR IS A YOUNGER MAN, HIS SON.
RALPH: Hi, this is Ralph Jones, and welcome to another chapter of the Jones Family Album.

2. MEDIUM SHOT — ANGLE ON OLDER MAN
NOW RALPH IS IN PROFILE, AND THE GUEST, STANLEY JONES, IS FULL FACE TO THE CAMERA.
RALPH: Today, it's my great pleasure and honor to have my father, Stanley Jones, on the show. Stanley was born in this very city many years ago, and he's brought along his own family photo album to show us some snapshots of his early years.

3. SLOW ZOOM — ZOOM IN ON FAMILY ALBUM TILL IT BECOMES A CLOSE UP.
STANLEY: This city has sure changed a lot since I was a boy.
HE OPENS THE ALBUM TO A SPECIFIC (PRE-PLANNED) PHOTO.
See this empty lot here? We used to play stickball in this lot. Now there's a shopping mall there.
THE CAMERA PANS AS HE POINTS TO ANOTHER PHOTO.
And here's my brother, your uncle, standing in a bean field. That bean field is where the new city hall was built in 1966.

(continued next page)

4. LONG SHOT — JONES FAMILY LIVING ROOM
ONCE AGAIN WE SEE BOTH RALPH AND STANLEY.
RALPH: What was the city like when you first moved here, in . . .
STANLEY: . . . 1947. I'll never forget it as long as I live.
CAMERA SLOWLY ZOOMS IN ON A CLOSE SHOT OF STANLEY'S FACE.
When we left our home back East, it had been snowing, and it was 5 below zero. When we got off the train here, it was 77 degrees, the sun was shining, and the whole place smelled like orange blossoms.
CAMERA PULLS BACK INTO A MEDIUM SHOT WITH RALPH AND STANLEY.
RALPH: Dad, I'd really like to see some more photos from the family album, but first, another member of our family has a short commercial message.
CUT TO:

5. MEDIUM SHOT — EXTERIOR. BOY STANDING NEXT TO LAWNMOWER. ELEVEN YEAR OLD TIMMY JONES ADDRESSES THE CAMERA.
TIMMY: Hi, this is Timmy Jones. This summer my parents said I could have a bicycle if I could make $50 mowing lawns, so I'd like to mow your lawn. I'm a hard worker, I'll bring my own mower over, and I'll do your whole yard for $2.00, or just a dollar for the front yard only.
CAMERA SLOWLY ZOOMS IN ON TIMMY'S FACE.
Just come by my house and say you want Timmy Jones to mow your lawn. Thanks a lot.
CUT TO:

6. LONG SHOT — JONES FAMILY LIVING ROOM
A RETURN TO THE SAME SET-UP AS THE BEGINNING.
RALPH: I understand you have a photograph of me when I was 8 years old, in front of Finley Park.

THE
END

7. MEDIUM SHOT — ANGLE ON OLDER MAN. ONCE AGAIN, WE SEE STANLEY OVER RALPH'S SHOULDER. HE OPENS HIS VIDEO ALBUM.
STANLEY: Yep, it's right here.
THE CAMERA ZOOMS IN ON A CLOSE SHOT OF A PHOTO IN THE ALBUM.
That was where the old minor league team, the Bulldogs, used to play their games. In fact, the day that I took this photograph, you got hit in the head with a foul ball.
RALPH: I remember that!
THE CAMERA PULLS BACK TO REVEAL STANLEY ONCE AGAIN IN A MEDIUM SHOT.
STANLEY: And after the game, we went down and had the ball autographed.

8. A LONG SHOT — COUCH IN LIVING ROOM
RALPH: I still have that baseball, right here (holds up ball). Well, that concludes this edition of the Jones Family Album. Next time, my guest will be Dorothy Jones, Stanley's wife and my mom, who will tell us all about her experiences as a Red Cross Nurse during World War II. Good bye!

CRITIQUE YOURSELF

14

**HOW TO BE
YOUR OWN BEST CRITIC**

The best way to learn video-making is by doing... and then reviewing. Once you know the basic rules and tools, you should practice making video stories as often as you can.

Review Yourself

After each production is completed, review it with your critical audience eye. "Mistakes" will jump right out at you. You'll see better ways to tell your story. Perhaps you missed an Establishing Shot. Maybe you used a Medium Shot when a Close Shot would have focused attention on an important detail. Did you cross the line without informing the audience? Did you miss a perfect opportunity to follow the action by Tracking?

Since videos consist of words and pictures, you may find that viewing the pictures with the sound off will help you concentrate on the shots you've taken. Without the distraction of the dialogue or sound effects, you can concentrate on how and when you used the Long, Medium and Close Shot. Did you use the Long Shot to establish the location and principal characters of your video? By now, you've probably found that the Medium Shot is your most frequently used "video tool." It's your normal or standard shot. It concentrates attention on the most important part of your subject; it let's you in on the action. What about your Close Shots? Are you using them effectively? Remember, the Close Shot adds description, color and interest to your story.

After you've made a few videos by following the "rules," try breaking them for effect. Instead of beginning with a Long Shot, try a Medium Shot or a Pan Shot to open. Even a Tracking Shot can be an effective opener. Your goal in the Opening Shot is to establish the "who, when and where" of your story. Try starting with a Close Shot and then slowly Zoom Out to reveal the setting of your video.

Critique your cuts. Notice how your sequence develops. Did you follow the "establish and build" principle? Your video should communicate a story or message. Did you make your point? Effectively? Every story has a beginning, a middle, and an end. Even a video of your vacation will consist of these three parts. And the story will be told by linking individual shots together. The more videos you make, the more confident and creative you'll become in telling a story. And don't be afraid of "cut to's." That's where your skill at in-camera editing will help you tell an effective, well-paced story. Long takes, while easy to make, can bore an audience to distraction. Unless there's really something happening during a shot, don't leave the camera rolling. Turn it off and go to the next shot.

There are very few rules for successful video making. Learn them and follow them. Good lighting. A sound track you can hear. A sharp, crisp picture. Good color. A story that is believable. A story that is portrayed by sincere participants. But most of all, a good story is well planned . . . in advance. For "happenings," a story outline will suffice. After awhile, you'll know which shots are best; which shots work in a given situation and which shots don't work. By experience, you'll instinctively go to the right camera positions and choose the best camera angles.

If you plan to "stage" a video, you'll need a script and a storyboard. You can use these "tools of the trade" not only to produce your video, but also to critique it once you're through with the production. These "tools" will serve as a guide as you review the video. Did you follow the storyboard or outline? If not, did you have a good reason to deviate?

Learning by reviewing will also help you make your next story outline or storyboard more effective. You know the old joke: "What's the best way to get to Carnegie Hall? Practice!" It's the same with video-making. The more you practice and critique, the better videos you'll make.

Look at Television

Learning a new subject usually requires that we attend school at some distant location. But as a video-maker, your teacher is as near as your television set.

Everytime you turn on your TV, you have access to the best video teachers in the world. Hundreds of thousands of dollars of talent and production go into the making of most TV shows. Use each of these shows as your teacher.

Notice how the director establishes the story; how he or she cuts from shot to shot to weave the story. See when the Long Shot, Medium Shot, or Close Shot is used to best effect. Notice when camera angles are changed. See how the director changes camera positions without crossing the line.

You'll be amazed to see how often Tracking Shots are used to liven up monologues. Notice the various lighting techniques used. Once you understand key, fill, back and background lighting, you'll instantly recognize how and when they're used.

See if you can tell how closely professional directors follow the rules of composition. You may be surprised to see how strictly the Rule of Thirds is adhered to.

For some really creative ideas, watch TV commercials. Directors of commercials are some of the most innovative and talented video-makers. They have learned how to tell a story concisely and completely... in 30 or 60 seconds! See how and when they Track; when and why they Zoom In or Zoom Out; how and when they use Close Shots. See how often they "Cut to" the next shot. Notice how well-lit their sets are. You can learn a great deal about video-making from TV commercials.

As with your own production, view the work of others with the sound off. This will allow you to concentrate on the pictures and how they relate to each other.

To learn more about how to create dialogue and sound effects, listen to TV shows with the picture turned off. You can eliminate the picture by simply rotating the "contrast" or "brightness" knob or control. As you listen, you'll be amazed at how little the actors really talk; how important music and sound effects are to creating a mood; and, most importantly, how vital the visuals are to a good story, documentary, news program, soap, and even to a music video.

Read On!

There are lots of good reading materials on video-making. One good source is your daily paper, T.V. Guide, and the T.V. section of national magazines. All contain reviews of TV shows and productions. See what the reviewer thinks is important. You can learn how to produce good video by reading these reviews.

There are also some good special interest, video enthusiast magazines. Many of them have a video-making tips feature each month. Read them, try out their suggestions, and you'll continually learn to make better videos.

GLOSSARY

Angle Of View — The angle of view refers to the quantity of a scene that will be captured by the lens. A wide angle lens will take in more of the scene than a normal or telephoto lens. The angle of view is determined by the focal length of a lens. A long focal length lens (a telephoto lens) will have a narrow angle of view. A short focal length lens (a wide angle lens) will have a wide angle of view.

Aperture — Refers to the adjustable hole that controls the amount of light passing through the lens. The aperture is controlled by a diaphragm. To let more light in, simply open the hole; to restrict the amount of light passing through the lens, simply close the hole down. The aperture works much like the pupil of the eye. It can be enlarged or contracted to suit the current lighting conditions. The amount of light passing through the lens and falling on the light sensitive tube or imaging chip not only controls the exposure but also determines the depth of focus or depth of field. Aperture is usually expressed as an f-stop, e.g., f1.8, f2.8, f16 etc.

Artificial Light — As distinguished from "natural light." Artificial light sources include every light source other than the sun. Most professional video productions use artificial light sources to illuminate the set and the actors. While many home video makers use artifical light, the vast majority are shot out-of-doors and therefore rely solely on natural light.

Assembly Editing — The rearranging of shots from a master tape by means of recording to another tape, known as an edit master, the result of which is the assembling of all the shots to be retained on a single tape and the discarding of the remaining shots.

Audio Dub — The process by which an existing audio track is replaced with another audio track. In the process, the existing track is erased and the new track is recorded "over" it.

Audio-Input/Output — The jack connections on VCR's which permits the receiving or delivery of the audio signal to or from the VCR.

Automatic Gain Control — The automatic adjusting of audio input levels during recording. Most cameras are equipped with AGC which permits the camera operator to be free from adjusting the sound level during recording and instead concentrate on the visuals. AGC causes the microphone to "reach out" and grab any sound within range. Its strength is therefore its weakness; it records any sound, whether desired or not.

Back Lighting — A lighting technique whereby the light source is placed behind the subject. This technique adds depth and dimension to the scene and makes the subject stand out from the background . . . an important technique when working in a two-dimensional media such as video.

Background Lighting — A lighting technique whereby the light source is aimed directly at the background. Its purpose is to illuminate the background or backdrop and, to add a "quality" look to the video.

Backdrop — Describes a curtain hung at the back of a stage or set. Often scenes will be painted on the curtain to depict time and/or place.

Beta — 1/2 inch VCR and tape format developed by Sony.

Bounce Lighting — A lighting technique whereby light is reflected off a wall, ceiling, lighting umbrella or some other large, light-colored surface. The purpose is to create a more even, indirect light which is more flattering than direct light. Direct light tends to create deep shadows. Where only a single light source is available, bounce lighting is the technique often selected.

Cable Television — Cable television is distinguished from broadcast television in that the latter transmits or broadcasts its signal over the air waves. Cable sends its signal to the viewer by a coaxial cable or wire. While many cable services send their signal by cable or wire on a fee basis, some pay "cable" services send their signal over the air. Although not literally a cable service, both actual cable and private, over-the-air services are known generically as "cable TV."

Cam-corder — Literally, the combining of the words "camera" and "recorder" to form a new word "cam-corder." The term describes a camera and recorder combined into one unit. Cam-corders come in the most popular formats, i.e., 1/2" VHS, Beta and the new 8mm format.

Capstan — The roller located in the VCR which determines and governs the speed of the tape transport. A Capstan Servo links the speed of two VCR's so that they are in synch during, for example, editing.

Cardiod — Describes the heart-shaped area in front of a cardiod microphone which is within its sound gathering range.

Character Generator — (See Special Effects Generator.)

Chroma Key — Chroma refers to the saturation of color in a video signal. Chroma Key is the replacement, by electronic means, of one color signal for another. The replacement color is almost always blue.

Close Shot — Describes a camera shot made close to the subject. The purpose of a Close Shot is to call the audience's attention to a single feature of the subject.

Color Bars — The standard for measuring the levels and phasings of original recordings and for adjusting the correct color reception of home television receivers. Color bars were developed as the industry standard by the Society of Motion Picture and Television Engineers (known in the trade as SMPTE). The test bars are accompanied by a 1,000 Hz audio sound for audio reference and adjustment. (See Hertz (Hz).)

Component — Any device that is or may be part of the electronic video recording or playback system.

Contrast — A lighting term used to describe the ratio between the lightest light and the darkest dark in a scene. While the human eye can "see" scenes of high contrast - the camera cannot "see" such a wide range of contrast. It may see a dark gray as a black or an ivory white as a brilliant white. Therefore, it is important to control the contrast ratio in every scene so that the camera may faithfully reproduce the true intensity of the colors.

Control Track — Video tape is made up of an audio track, a video track and a control track, all running the length of the tape. The control track contains speed control pulses which serve to set the speed of the tape on playback by controlling the recorder. Control track information is read by the control track head on the VCR.

Convergence — The process by which the three primary colors, red, blue and green, overlap to create a color image.

Copyright — A body of laws which protect the "original" works of authors, composers and artists from copying. "Work" refers to the product of the creator's efforts; an author's work would be a book; a composer's work would be a musical composition, song or score; an artist's work would be a painting or sculpture; a television writer's work would be a script; a television producer's work would be a completed edited master tape; and so on. This body of copyright law vests in the owner of the work the exclusive right to control the copying and performance of the results of his or her creative efforts. While each country has its own body of copyright laws, together they provide a web of international protection by means of treaties between nations.

CRT — Cathode Ray Tube. From the inception of television, the standard television picture tube.

Cut To — This is a directorial term to the camera operator to stop shooting the current scene and "cut to," or commence shooting the next scene in the shooting sequence.

Definition — A subjective measure of picture sharpness and resolution.

Depth Of Field — Also known as depth of focus. The term describes the range - from foreground to background - on which the lens is focused. Depth of focus is determined by the f-stop, or aperture. If the aperture is wide-open (f1.4), depth of focus will be narrow; if the lens is stopped-down (f16), the lens will have everything in front of it, from close foreground to background, in sharp focus. Thus, aperture not only controls exposure, but also depth of focus.

Dissolve — Describes fading out of one scene and into another.

Distortion — A form of electronic noise or electronic interference with the video signal.

Dolby — A patented system for reducing the noise inherent in recording tape. Other noise reduction systems exist, but Dolby appears to be the most popular and widely used.

Drop-Out — The momentary loss of a video or audio signal.

Dub — Literally means to duplicate or copy. In audio or video, dubbing is accomplished by connecting a playback machine to a recorder and recording or copying the material from the playback unit to the recording unit.

Edit — The process by which original video material is prepared for final viewing by selecting, arranging, re-arranging and deleting from the original taped material (the master) in order to create the desired final "edited" master.

Editing Controller — An electronic device which facilitates both insert and assembly editing by permitting precise control over edit points. Sophisticated models permit the editor to rehearse each edit by means of a preview edit feature, thereby ensuring perfect edits.

Edited Master — The edited master is actually a copy of the master tape which has been assembled or edited from the master in order to create the final viewing product. The edited master is a first generation copy or dub.

Eisenstein's Law — An editing principle which states that two images placed next to each other will create an entirely different third image in the mind of the viewer.

Electronic Viewfinder — A miniture tv receiver included as part of the video camera in which the image is generated by a CRT. The electronic viewfinder allows the camera operator to view the scene to be videotaped precisely as it will be seen on television during the playback.

Erase Head — The head on a VCR which is used for the purpose of erasing previously recorded material.

Establishing Shot — Another term for the Long Shot. When referred to as an Establishing Shot, it describes that the Long Shot is used to establish the subject and place of the action in a video production.

Fade — To cause an image to appear or disappear gradually. In video making, fade-in means gradually bringing the scene up to view; fade-out means gradually bringing the scene into black, out of view of the audience.

Fill Lighting — A lighting technique whereby a subject lit with a Key Light is also lit with a Fill Light in order to mould the subject and to fill in the shadows created by the Key Light. Fill Light is of far less intensity than the Key Light.

Film Chain — Also known as a Telecine. A video camera combined with a film projector which is used to transfer film or slides to video.

Flat — A piece of theatrical scenery painted on a flat frame.

Focal Length — A lens is measured by its focal length. A long focal length lens is commonly referred to as a telephoto lens, whereas a lens of short focal length is referred to as a wide-angle lens. Focal length is a measure of the distance between the optical center of the lens to the surface of the vidicon tube or solid-state imager when the lens is set at infinity. In film cameras, focal length is a measure of the distance between optical center of the lens to the film surface. Thus, in both film and video, focal length measures the distance from optical center of the lens to the recording or "seeing" surface of the camera, the tube in video and the film plane in film cameras.

Focus — To adjust the camera lens so that it will produce a sharp, clear, distinct image on the light sensitive tube or imaging chip.

Foot Candles — The measure of light falling on a surface. The term describes the amount of light projected from one hypothetical candle falling on one square foot of a pure white surface from a distance of one foot. The light sensitivity of a camera's tube or solid-state imager may be expressed in "foot candles." As such, it will mean the minimum number of foot candles required to produce an acceptable image with the manufacturer's camera model. (Also see Lux.)

Frame — Describes one complete tv picture. In video, the frame is comprised of two electronic fields; in film, the frame is comprised of one still image recorded on film. The frame rate is measured in seconds. Video and film frame rates are different, which is why a video of a film that is broadcast over television flickers.

Freeze Frame — An optional feature offered by many VCR's which allows the viewer to stop and yet still maintain an image on the tv screen. Without this feature, stopping the tape will normally result in lack of any image on the screen.

F-stop — Refers to the size of the aperture or lens opening. Aperture sizes are referred to as f-stops. It is a worldwide standard for measuring the amount of light passing through the lens. The commonly used f-stop numbers are: fl.4, f2, f2.8, f4, f5.6, f8, f11, f16, and f22. Starting from the widest lens aperture, fl.4, each larger number reduces the amount of light passing through the lens by exactly one-half. So that by using f2.0, you will let one-half the amount of light through the lens as you did when using f1.4, and so on. Conversely, the smaller the number, the larger the aperture.

Gain — A measure of the degree of amplification of an electronic signal. In video, it is a measure of the whiteness or luminance level of a video image.

Gel — A lighting term used as a shorthand expression of "gelation." A Gel is used as a color filter which is placed over a white light source in order to provide a desired light color. For example, a blue Gel placed over a white light source provides a blue light.

Generation — Refers to the ancestry of the tape. The original tape is referred to as the "master." If post production editing is done, the resulting tape is called the "edited master." Tape copies, or dubs, made from the master or the edited master are the "generations." For example, the first copies made directly from the master are called first generation tapes. Copies made from the first generation are called second generation copies . . . and so on. Substantial video quality is lost with each succeeding generation.

Glitch — Tv industry shorthand for any electronic distortion or defect in a video image or picture.

Graphics — Refers to the drawings, illustrations, diagrams, titles, and art-work that are used in video productions to identify the opening, closing, and production credits. Graphics also refers to the visual aids used in the taping of a production to highlight or illustrate the topic, e.g., a sales chart which visually illustrates the speaker's topic.

Hand Held — Describes a method of supporting the camera, and is distinguished from tripod or monopod support.

Hardware — Video equipment is referred to as hardware, while tape, books, and other media supplying the information upon which the hardware is run are referred to as software.

Head — An integral part of the VCR; the electromagnetic device which converts electronic signals on the tape to audio or video images on the screen. Heads can be "playback heads," "record heads," or "erase heads." Erase heads wipe out or erase the electromagnetic signals, while record heads place these signals, on tape where they remain until erased.

Helical Scan — Describes the method of recording electronic images by a VCR whereby the rotating drum records a long diagonal series of tracks from the video heads to the tape which is moving in a lateral direction across the drum.

Hertz — Hertz is a measure of the cycles per second of radio or electromagnetic waves. Hertz is an internationally used standard. The measurement was developed by H. R. Hertz, a German physicist who died in 1894.

Hue — Refers to the overall color emphasis of the taped production. The overall hue will be derived from one of the primary colors of the video image; red, green or blue. If the video image appearing on the screen is primarily greenish, blueish or reddish, the fault may be a monitor maladjustment or the lighting conditions prevailing at the time the production was shot. The color of the lighting may be affected by the color temperature of the light source. (See Kelvin.)

Hum — Refers to a low frequency noise which is audible during playback.

Image Enhancer — An electronic hardware device which assists in sharpening a video image.

Image Plane — The surface of the tube behind the lens on which the image is in sharp focus.

Insert Editing — To be distinguished from Assembly Editing. Through the use of an electronic editing device, the replacement of one scene on a tape for a new scene; the new scene is "inserted" in place of the old one.

Iris — Also known as the "diaphragm." It is the device which controls the aperture setting of the lens. The aperature setting, in turn, controls both exposure and depth of focus. (See Depth of Field.)

Kelvin — Is the standard measure of the color temperature of light. Many cameras are equipped with a color temperature switch which permits adjustment for indoor and outdoor shooting, since indoor and outdoor lighting are each of a different color temperature. Artificial lights, such as flourescent, are greenish in overall hue; quartz halogen lights are harshly white; while ordinary incandescent or household bulbs cast a slightly warm, white tone. The sun is said to cast a blueish colored light.

Key Lighting — The main light source in a video production. Normally, the Key Light is placed in front of the subject, positioned off to one side, and raised above the subject. Placement off to the side tends to "shape" the subject by casting shadows and creating contrast. The Key Light is a narrow, focused light which highlights and features the subject.

Keying — The matteing or placing of one video image over another video image.

Lag — Occurs when shooting in low light. Lag is a ghost image which is momentarily retained by the vidicon tube. The viewer sees the retained image as well as the new image; the retained image temporarily "lags" behind.

Lavalier Microphone — Also known as the "personal" microphone. It is a tiny microphone worn around the neck or pinned to an article of clothing. It is often used on interview or "talk" shows.

Level — Describes the volume or strength of an audio or video signal.

Lux — Like Foot Candles, Lux is a measure of light sensitivity. Lux is one lumen per square meter. One Foot Candle is equal to 10.76 Lux. The sensitivity of a camera's tube or solid-state imager may be expressed by the manufacturer in either foot candles or lux.

Line, The — Refers to an imaginary line created by the action, or the placement of the actors, or the direction in which the camera is pointed. Once the line is created in the mind of the viewer, it is a principle of film or video making that the line not be crossed in such a way as would confuse the audience.

Line Scan — Refers to the sweep of the electron beam across the picture tube during each picture frame. There is no international standard line scan. Instead, there are three competing standards. In the United States and Japan, the NTSC (National Television Standards Commission) standard is used. It calls for 525 line scans per frame. In many European countries the PAL, (Phase Alternating Line) standard is used. It calls for 625 line scans per frame and provides more picture detail and resolution. Other countries use still a third standard. The standards are incompatible. A tape recorded on the NTSC system may not be played back on the PAL system. It must first be converted by re-recording on a machine using the compatible system.

Long Shot — Describes a shot by the camera operator where the camera is positioned a sufficient distance from the subject so as to "take in" both the subject and his or her surroundings. (See the Establishing Shot.)

Long Take — An alternative to the normal way of shooting, i.e., shooting a scene by means of inter-cutting between Long, Medium and Close Shots. In the Long Take, the camera continues to roll as the camera operator moves around to various camera positions and shoots the entire scene without interruption and without inter-cutting.

Luminance — The term used to describe the intensity of brightness of a picture tube.

Macro Lens — A close-up lens which works like a magnifying lens. Many video cameras come equipped with a macro lens which is integrated into the camera lens.

Megahertz (MHz) — One million Hertz.

Medium Shot — Can be described as the camera being positioned between what would be called a Long Shot and a Close Shot. The Medium Shot is used to concentrate the viewer on the most important aspect of the action taking place in front of the camera. This is probably the most often used shot in video productions.

Mixer — A piece of hardware which allows the user to mix electronic signals coming from different sources and thereby create a new, integrated, mixed signal onto a composite track. In recording music, electronic signals from two or more microphones are fed into a mixer where they are "mixed" together to form an integrated electronic signal.

Monitor — A monitor is a television which has not been equipped with a tuner. A receiver, on the other hand, is a monitor equipped with a tuner. Professional studios and television production facilities normally use a monitor to "monitor" the results of the current production. Homes usually find it more practical to use a receiver to preserve the wide choice of viewing channels available.

Ni-cad — Refers to a battery made of nickel cadmium which is used to power portable cameras and VCR's.

Noise — Noise is any kind of electronic interference which affects the recording or play back of the video signal. Noise includes both distortion and snow.

Omni-Directional Microphone — A microphone which picks up sound from all directions. Contrast with a uni-directional mike which picks up sound from only one direction.

One Tube Color Camera — Home video cameras come equipped with one tube which is designed to pick up the three primary colors — red, green and blue. Professional broadcast cameras come equipped with three tubes, one for each of the primary colors.

Panning — Whenever the camera, located in a fixed position, is moved horizontally from right-to-left or left-to-right during a shot, a Pan Shot is produced.

Pause Control — A switch located on most cameras which permits the pause feature on the VCR to be operated directly from the camera. The pause control stops the tape, yet allows the motor to keep running. Thus, when the pause control is depressed, the tape stops; when it is depressed again, the tape starts recording without any loss in recording which would otherwise occur due to the delay in motor start-up time.

Photoflood Bulb — An inexpensive light bulb used for video productions as artificial lighting for shooting indoors.

Production Periods — The time periods or phases of a video production can be divided in three: Pre-Production phase refers to the time in which a production is readied for shooting — all of the tasks required to begin shooting are accomplished during the pre-production phase; Production refers to the actual shooting period; and Post Production refers to the time in which the tape is readied for release or final viewing by the audience.

Pre-Roll — Describes the set-up of the tape in the editing controller in preparation for an electronic edit.

Primary Colors — Color television pictures are made up of three primary colors; red, blue and green. The convergence or mixture of these primary colors results in a perfect tv color image. (See Convergence.)

Program — A generic term which refers to a tv presentation such as a movie, a concert, a stage play, a documentary, or a production made especially for television such as a drama or comedy.

Programmable VCR — An optional feature available on most VCR's that allows the viewer to pre-set the recording of tv broadcasts which will take place at some future time. For example, an 8 program/21 day optional recording feature permits the recording of 8 different programs over a 21 day period. Programmable recording is controlled by an internal timer located in the VCR.

Props — Short for "properties"; describes any of the movable articles used as part of the setting except costumes, flat, and backdrops.

Public Domain — Under the law of most countries, copyright protects an original work for the life of the author or composer plus an additional period of 50 years after his or her death. During the period of copyright, the owner may control the copying and performance of his work and may collect royalties for its use. Once the copyright period passes, however, the work may be used without consent and without payment. After expiration of the copyright, the work is said to pass into the public domain.

Quartz Lighting — The use of quartz halogen bulbs to produce high intensity lighting of the subject matter. Quartz light guns are a popular form of artificial lighting among video enthusiasts.

Raw Stock — Refers to new, unused video tape or film which is ready to be used for a video or film production.

RGB — A shorthand description of the primary video colors (red, green, and blue.)

Resolution — A description of the sharpness of the video picture.

Roll — A defect in the video image caused by momentary loss of vertical synch.

Rule Of Thirds — A rule of composition which provides that a picture achieves an artful balance and a pleasing presentation when the camera frame is divided in thirds, both hortizontally and vertically. By dividing the frame into thirds, the camera operator will have a guide to proper placement of his subjects within the frame to achieve a pleasing composition.

Saticon Tube — A video tube made from arsenic tellurium. The saticon tube provides less lag than the conventional and more widely used vidicon tube.

Saturation — Color saturation refers to the intensity of color in a video image.

Scene — A part of a video production which constitutes a unit of development or action during which the action is continuous and there is no shift in time.

Script — The second stage in the planning of a video production (after the story outline). A script is made up of three parts: the diaglogue; stage directions; and, a short description of the shots to be made by the camera operator.

Set — Describes the arrangement of backdrops, flats, props, etc., constructed and assembled for a scene in a video production.

Selective Focus — Setting the focus on one particular element in the composition while allowing all other elements to remain out of focus. Selective focus can best be accomplished by using a telephoto lens.

Signal To Noise Ratio — The "signal" carries the picture, while the "noise" is electronic interference with the picture. Thus, the higher the signal to noise ratio, the better the picture quality. Noise is produced by the equipment which reproduces the picture or signal. Equipment which features a high signal to noise ratio is to be preferred.

Software — As distinguished from "hardware," software refers to the information contained in the media in which it is stored. For example, a rock concert (or any tv program) preserved on a video cassette is generically referred to as software.

Solid-State Imager — A solid-state electronic chip, lately developed to replace the vidicon tube. It is smaller than the tube and therefore permits the manufacture of smaller cameras. However, it is not as sensitive to light as the tube and therefore will not record in extremely low light. Solid-state refers to any device made up of transistors or micro-chips in the place of vacuum tubes.

Snow — A form of electronic interference. Snow on the screen looks like a snowstorm of white snowflakes drifting across the screen. Snow interferes with the electronic tv signal being broadcast or played back on the monitor or receiver.

Special Effects — The term covers a myriad of effects which may be generated electronically, including alphanumeric characters, titles, graphics, and various electronic effects such as positive/negative reversal, which enhance a video production.

Special Effects Generator — A hardware device which creates various special effects and permits the mixing or switching of these effects into the main video signal. Many cameras have Special Effects Generators built-in; Character Generators can be used to create alphanumeric characters for titles and graphics; Day/Time Switch allows the camera operator to record the day and time directly onto the video tape cassette; Positive/Negative Reversal can be used by the camera operator to create reverse images on tape as a special effect.

Story Outline — The first step in planning a video production. The story outline is a summary of the story or production, set out in a logical, progressive format.

Storyboard — The last step (after a story outline and a script) in planning a video production. A storyboard is a visual illustration, or pictorial guide, of the production, much like the frames of a comic strip.

Switcher — The switcher is a piece of hardware into which the output of two or more cameras is fed, thereby enabling the smooth transition of scenes shot by one camera into shots made by the other camera. If the switcher is equipped with a fader, it will facilitate the gradual transition from one camera to the other.

Synch — Short for synchronization. Describes the vertical and horizontal pulses that are synchronized to coordinate a television scanning system.

Tape — Both video and audio tape are made of oxide which is bonded to a backing. Oxide, which is made up of magnetic particles, is now being replaced by metal and metal evaporated materials for better sound and video recording and reproduction with less tape hiss. Whether oxide or metal, recording tape permits the recording of electronic pulses which, when played back, produce audible sound and visual images.

Tape Generation — Designates a tape by its lineage, such as a "master," "first generation," "second generation," etc., copy or dub. The farther down the line, the more distortion with resultant poorer picture quality.

Tearing — A kind of distortion visible on playback of the video tape caused when horizontal synch is lost or distorted.

Tilt — A shooting technique where the camera is tilted up during operation. It is also described as a vertical Pan Shot. Its purpose is to communicate height in a way that no static shot can.

Time Code — Reference points inserted in each frame by means of recording the code on the spare video tape track. Especially useful in video editing.

Time Shift — Refers to the primary use of VCR's; the ability to record a program for later viewing. Until 1984, time shifting in the United States was prohibited by law, since the right to tape off the air tv broadcasts was deemed a violation of copyright law. However, in that year, the U.S. Supreme Court declared that home taping of tv broadcasts for private use was permitted under the copyright laws of the United States. Notwithstanding the pronouncements of the U.S. Supreme Court, home taping is still a violation of the copyright laws of most other countries. Numerous surveys have shown that time shift is the primary use of home VCR's.

Tracking — A shooting technique which involves the camera moving during operation. The Tracking Shot is used to add drama, impact and immediacy to the action. It also creates a sense of "action" when there otherwise would be none, e.g., where the camera tracks a stationary speaker.

Transmission — The transmitting or broadcast of electronic signals over the air waves.

Tuner — An electro-mechanical device which adjusts the frequency or channel received by a radio or television. Radio frequencies include AM and FM, while television frequencies include VHF and UHF. Each frequency requires its own tuner.

UHF — The Ultra-High Frequency of the broadcast band. On most tv's, UHF channels include those from 14 through 83.

VCR — The standard abbreviation for video cassette recorder. Also known as the VTR, video tape recorder. Professional models are known as "U-Matic" (a tradename of Sony) and use a 3/4 inch tape cassette. Home models are now available in 3 formats: both VHS and Beta use the 1/2 inch format, while the latest development, 8mm, uses a tape which is 8mm, or approximately 1/4 inch wide. The VCR is the hardware upon which the software (video tape cassette) may be played to produce a viewing image on the tv screen.

VHF — The Very High Frequency of the broadcast band. On most tv's, VHF channels include those from 2 through 13.

VHS — The 1/2" video format offered as an alternative to Beta. Although both using 1/2" tape, Beta and VHS are incompatible systems.

Video — Creating images by electronic means.

Videocassette — A housing for video tape which permits the recording and play back of the video tape without hands, dirt, etc., coming in contact with the tape.

Vidicon Tube — The most commonly used pick-up tube in video cameras. Alternate means of video pick-up include the Saticon tube and the solid-state imager.

Viewfinder — The camera device through which the camera operator may see that which is visible to the lens and through which he may compose and focus the picture. Viewfinders are electronic or optical.

White Balance — The system of color balance used in video cameras to balance color temperature so that the camera reproduces true color images. The system is based on obtaining a true white.

Windscreen — A baffle made of foam, placed over the microphone head to reduce the sound of wind which may be present during outdoor recording.

Wipe — A video special effect whereby one image is replaced by another. To the viewer it appears as if the new image is "wiped" on the screen, thereby "wiping off" the old image.

Zoom Lens — A variable focal length lens which is capable of "zooming" from wide-angle to telephoto, or vice-versa, while the camera is running and the VCR is recording.

Zooming — A Zoom Shot; a shot in which the focal length of the lens is altered during the shot.

ABOUT THE AUTHORS

Robert Hirschman

Robert Hirschman earns his living as a writer of sorts. He has an extensive background in photography, having attended one of the most prestigious art schools in the country, Art Center College of Design in Los Angeles, California. He is also a graduate of California State University and holds a Juris Doctor from the University of California, Hastings College of the Law.

As the creator of Videoware's "How to Shoot" series, Robert Hirschman brings an unusual depth of understanding to the amateur and semi-pro video maker and photographer. Coupled with his understanding of the needs of both new and experienced video makers is Hirschman's ability to explain each point in this Videoware series in a clear, concise, easy-to-read manner. This comes from years of trial and error experimentation. In other words, he fumbled around so you don't have to!

Richard Procter

Richard Procter, a graduate of the English Department of the University of California at Santa Barbara, is one of the talented new breed of Hollywood writers currently working his way to the top. Following graduation from UCSB, Procter participated in the graduate film-making program at UCLA. He has extensive creative writing experience, and brings both creativity and hands-on knowledge to Videoware's unique series of books on video making.

His television writing includes network shows such as "Newhart," "Domestic Life" and "People Are Funny." He has also developed projects for the HBO and Showtime Cable Networks, including "Video Showdown" and "Dreamweaver."

Procter is an avid video buff; he owns an extensive collection of movies on video, especially Hollywood comedies of the '30's and '40's.